the litt**le book of** LIKES

Social Media
for Small
(And Very Small)
Nonprofits

by Erik Hanberg

The Little Book of Likes
Social Media for Small and Very Small Nonprofits
By Erik Hanberg
Copyright © 2013 by Erik Hanberg

ISBN-13: 978-0-9827145-5-3

TABLE OF CONTENTS

Introduction

EVERY DAY, WE hear that some new piece of technology or a social media site is going to revolutionize our daily lives. And every day, life moves on pretty much as it did the day before. We get up, we have coffee, we go to work. The only difference is now people are tweeting about it, right?

To an extent, yes. A lot of people on Twitter or Facebook are talking about the sandwich they just ate. But it would be a shame to ignore an entire means of communication because of the inane conversations that occur on it. If we were to judge all communications by that standard, we'd never make phone calls either.

Social media is now a basic means of communication. Not that long ago, if your nonprofit didn't have a phone number, people would have been surprised. If you wanted to do business, you had to have one. Then you had to have an answering machine.

Then it was a website.

Now it's Facebook.

Your nonprofit needs to be on Facebook and Twitter in the same way that your nonprofit needs a phone number.

Perhaps you've picked up this book because you're already convinced you need a better social media presence; you're just not sure how to start. That's great! But for those who are still on the fence, I hope you will allow me a few paragraphs to spell out why social media is so important.

Why You Need to Be on Social Media

Social media is like a big party at your neighbor's house. From where you sit, it seems loud and obnoxious, and you wonder why anyone would bother going. But when you show up, you see some old friends, you meet some new people who share your interests, and you get to tell them a little more about yourself. The party turns out to be surprisingly fun and when you get home that night, you're glad you made yourself go.

There are very good reasons your nonprofit should embrace social media—why you should be at your neighbor's party:

- *Your donors are there.* No, maybe not the big ones, and maybe not many of them (yet). But they're there. There are a billion people on Facebook: I'm guessing at least a few of them are your donors. And don't judge just by age! Plenty of seniors join Facebook to see pictures of grandkids and then stick around when they realize it's fun.

- *Your potential donors are there too.* Social media is a great way to build an audience of people who care about your organization. Those people may not be current donors, but social media is a great way to put your message in front of them consistently and effectively. That's how you'll get them to give later.

- *Eavesdropping.* Almost certainly, people are talking about your organization on social media. Wouldn't it be nice to hear what they had to say? Or even have the chance to respond to them, *especially* if they have a complaint? Social media is an excellent tool to show the world your customer service skills.

- *Storytelling.* Your nonprofit may not be trying to change the world. Maybe there's just one small corner of it you want to make a little nicer. Telling stories about the good work you do in pursuit of your mission has never been easier … or cheaper.

Hopefully, we're now all in agreement: Yes, your nonprofit needs to be using social media. But how? Should you be on Facebook? Foursquare? Flickr? What questions should you even ask when trying to make that decision? Once you've picked a site, how often should you use it? What should you say?

So many questions! So little time.

This book will help your nonprofit answer those questions—and provide you a framework for evaluating new ideas or social media sites as they come up. Written for the executive director of a small nonprofit, this book assumes that you have many other things on your mind than updating your nonprofit's Facebook page. So my focus is on providing a road map for using social media effectively in a way that will scale with your organization's staffing levels and integrate with what you already do, from an executive director who's been there.

My Story

Most of my professional career has been in nonprofit fundraising, marketing, and management. That experience has come in all shapes and sizes. I've worked in fundraising for a large multimillion dollar nonprofit; run marketing initiatives for another; and led two nonprofits: an art-house movie theater and a small civic nonprofit.

But I have a "social" story as well, and it eventually intersects with my professional life.

One year, my dad, my wife, and I made a New Year's resolution to go to every park in my hometown of Tacoma, Washington. We took pictures, discovered new neighborhoods we hadn't visited before and, in general, learned a whole lot about our community. I thought that others might like to share in the experience, so I started a blog to chronicle the parks we saw, posting photos and our short reviews.

I was hooked. After I'd finished blogging about the parks, I started blogging about other things I liked: movies, travel, random bits of news. This was still very early in the social media days—not everyone had started blogging yet—and it was still rather novel. I kept at it, and my experience was enough that in 2006 I started writing on the side for a popular "hyperlocal" site in Tacoma that covered community news. Eventually I became a partner in that business and worked with a small team to produce great blog content for thousands of daily readers.

I saw the potential of social media for the nonprofits I led too. I did everything I could to increase their visibility on social media. At the nonprofit art-house movie theater, I launched a blog and signed up the staff as the bloggers to review movies—patrons always wanted to know "what's good this week" and this was a perfect way to tell them. At the small civic nonprofit, I launched a Twitter account and live-tweeted our programs such as political debates and forums on major issues. By showing people what they were missing, we made them interested in attending another program in the future.

Things came full circle in 2011, when I ran for public office. I campaigned to be a commissioner for Metro Parks Tacoma—the very park board that oversaw all the parks I'd visited and blogged about so many years before. That's when, personally speaking at least, my dedication to social media paid off. The relationships I'd formed online and the energy I'd put into posting about my love of Tacoma and its parks meant that when I was running for election, I already had a significant base of people who had heard of me and knew my passion for parks. As a result, my online appeals asking people to give to the campaign were surprisingly effective. Because I had put in the time.

Done right, social media can help your organization (and you) in a hundred different ways. My election story is a small example, but I hope it serves to illuminate the larger message:

If you care about something—like the mission of your nonprofit—you should share that passion with people online, and I promise you it will spread.

Meet "Linda"

In 2009, I wrote *The Little Book of Gold: Fundraising for Small (And Very Small) Nonprofits*. The book is a guide to basic fundraising principles as they apply to small nonprofits with shoestring budgets. To share the different techniques and processes, I decided to tell it as a story. So I created "Linda," the executive director of the Smallville Historical Society in Smallville, USA.

In my experience, stories are always more interesting and memorable than just a list of steps (although we'll have a few of those too). So we're going to stick with Linda's story and follow her first foray into social media.

Since we last saw her, Linda has had a few successful years of fundraising using practical and professional techniques. The budget of the Historical Society has stabilized thanks to her good work, and she's been able to expand the hours at the society's historic pioneer cabin and increase off-site education, such as more visits to elementary schools.

And yet ... why does she feel that 9 out of 10 people she runs into still have never heard of the Historical Society?

Linda has a tight marketing budget, and a lot of it was already committed. What can she do to get the word out about the Historical Society and the pioneer cabin? We're about to find out.

CHAPTER 1
Laying the Foundation

LINDA CAME IN to work frustrated. The night before, she'd met the mayor of Smallville at an event and had had a chance to tell him about the most recent exhibit at the Historical Society. He asked a lot of questions and was fascinated by everything she told him.

For a while, Linda felt good that she'd been able to tell the mayor of her hometown so much about the nonprofit she loved. But eventually she started to really think about the questions the mayor had asked her: "Where is the pioneer cabin again?" … "What kind of artifacts do you have there?" … "Do you have regular hours?"

She hadn't noticed it while she was answering the questions, but the implication was clear: The mayor had never been to the pioneer cabin. Worse, she wasn't entirely sure he'd *heard* of the Historical Society before she'd met him last night.

How was that even possible? He was the mayor of the town; wasn't he supposed to know everything about it? She was frustrated at him for not knowing about it, but by the next morning, she'd transferred her frustration to herself. It wasn't the mayor's fault he hadn't heard of the Historical Society; it was hers. If she wanted the mayor—and everyone else in Smallville—to know about the Historical Society, then it was up to her to get the word out.

But how? She didn't have much in the year's marketing budget. She could try to increase it in the next budget cycle, but until then, what could she do?

Social media maybe? Linda logged into her personal Facebook account and posted a status update: "Special Facebook offer! Come to the pioneer cabin today and mention Facebook, to get a 2-for-1 rate!"

She felt a little better. Linda got to work on a grant report to the state and didn't think about her marketing woes for the rest of the day.

Only when she came in the next day did she realize that she'd entirely forgotten to tell the staff at the pioneer cabin that she'd posted a special offer. When the cabin opened a few hours later, she checked in and asked if there'd been any issues with someone wanting the offer.

No issues at all ... because no one had asked for it.

She logged back into Facebook and saw that two people had "liked" her status. Both were family members who lived outside Smallville. No one else seemed to have paid the post any attention.

Linda drummed her fingers on the desk. "I thought social media was supposed to be so useful!" she said to the empty room.

This time, though, Linda didn't give up. She spent several hours finding the blogs, Twitter accounts, and Facebook pages of other Historical Societies around the country and studied them carefully. She looked at the pages of big national museums, and even though a lot of them seemed to have fancy videos and other features she didn't think she could produce, she got enough inspiration from them that she filled several pages with notes and ideas.

By the end of the day, she felt much more confident that she could put social media to good use. In those notes were the foundations for a simple plan that would match her small staff and limited budget.

The Plan

Linda didn't want to just post random promotions. She'd already tried that, and it clearly hadn't worked at all. She decided to sketch out a rough plan. Any plan was better than no plan, she figured.

So what was her goal? That was obvious: She wanted more people to come to the pioneer cabin and to learn about the Historical Society. That meant getting more people to hear about it, and more people to find it interesting enough to come. She wrote her goal at the top of the page.

At the bottom she wrote, "I will know this was successful when …"

When *what*? How would she know? Because attendance increased? Maybe. She wanted something more specific, though.

She thought about her conversation with the mayor and how frustrated it had made her. It was *that* conversation that she didn't want to repeat. She wanted people to light up with excitement when she told them where she worked, not get confused and ask which street it was on. So she finished the sentence:

"I will know this was successful when five strangers tell me *unasked* that they heard about us from social media."

That should be a good goal, she thought. And maybe a little ambitious.

But it still wasn't enough for her. She scribbled below it: "Secret Goal: I want the mayor to join the Historical Society as a member."

It seemed silly to put down on paper, but the truth of it was, that was what she really wanted. She wasn't sure how she would do it. But she was going to get him to join. And not just join. He was going to join willingly, without her even having to ask, with excitement and joy about the Historical Society.

Keeping it Focused

But how to do it?

What had she learned looking at all those other museums?

She needed a place to start: a hub for everything she was about to do. The website for the Historical Society was fine, but it didn't change very often. She needed a place to send people that would have new information, pictures, and more.

Linda decided she would create a blog. She'd never blogged before, but she regularly read two or three of them for fun and thought she had a good idea of how to do it. The blog would serve as a place she could put up interesting things about the Historical Society and the pioneer cabin. She imagined posting pictures of different artifacts from their collection, plus historical photos and the stories behind them, and she would sprinkle in information about upcoming events.

It would be great, she thought. Until a little voice in the back of her head asked, "*Why would anyone want to read about something as boring as this?*"

She paused and thought about it. That little voice had a point. It *did* have the potential to be really dry and boring. History was literally old news, and if it focused too much on dates and … well, the *boring* parts, no one would care.

But Linda loved this stuff. And whenever she told her friends about particularly interesting things in Smallville's history or exhibits that were featured at the cabin, they seemed genuinely engaged. She hoped she could make it interesting to people online too.

Oh! She just had an idea. Maybe she could interview some of the historical re-enactors in costume and in character. If she had a video camera and a tripod … OK, maybe this was already getting too complicated.

Keep it simple, she reminded herself. She didn't want to bite off more than she could chew. She would write three blog posts a week: two about history and one about museum events or programs. She thought she could maintain that volume.

Once she decided to blog, Linda turned to the list of social media services other museums used to see what else she should be doing. There were so many of them! Some used Pinterest and Foursquare and YouTube (and plenty more she'd never even heard of). And sometimes they were really interesting and inspiring. But she didn't think she had the time to spend on all of them. So she decided she would focus on two of the most common platforms to reach new people: Twitter and Facebook.

Those three services—a blog, Twitter, and Facebook—would form the core of her plan:

- Write a blog post.
- Share the link on Twitter and Facebook.
- Respond to comments.
- Invite blog readers to subscribe to an email newsletter.
- Repeat.

Once she got that going consistently, she'd consider other ideas, but for now, that was her plan. It's a simple plan that will work for your organization as well.

Why Is This Simple Plan So Effective?

We're going to cover the basics of each part of this plan and how to implement it, but we should spend a little time talking about *why* this is effective.

The first reason is that this plan is simple to understand: Write something, and then share it. Too many social media strategies can get overly complex and time-consuming. But don't be fooled by the simplicity of the strategy. Implementing it well means getting a dozen different details right during the process (all of which we'll cover in the coming pages).

The second reason this plan is so effective is that you are fulfilling a few different goals with the same action. A good blog post can emotionally connect with your readers and donors. It can get shared and re-shared on Facebook. It can positively affect your search result ranking on Google.

All of that means more interest in your nonprofit: more people signing up for your email newsletter, more people attending your events, more people aware of who you are when they need your services.

That's a lot of great benefits from just one short piece of writing.

The third reason this plan is effective is the final step: encouraging readers to sign up for an email newsletter. Why is this so important? Because—for a small nonprofit—social media can't be viewed as an end point in and of itself. Getting an email address from a reader is the door to turning that reader into a volunteer or a donor. Can it happen directly from Facebook? Yes, of course. But email will be much more effective. When it comes time to make an "ask" and turn readers into donors, you're going to do much better with an email than you are with just a Facebook post.

We're going to go through the basics of setting up the tools you will need to make this plan work, but as we get into those details, try not to lose the forest for the trees. Good social media leads to clicks, which leads to email addresses, which leads to donors and volunteers, which leads to you being better able to fulfill your nonprofit's mission.

CHAPTER 2
Creating a
Great Blog

BEFORE WE GO any further with Linda's story, we have to cover a very important point. This is a social media *strategy* book. The mechanics of it—specific questions like "Where should I click to update my Facebook cover photo?"—will not be addressed here.

First, if you already know the basics of navigating a social media site like Facebook, then all that description is going to bore you and you'll miss the important stuff.

Second, the answers to these kinds of questions change regularly as sites like Facebook and Twitter update their systems.

And third ... a book is a terrible way to teach those skills.

With all that in mind, I've worked with a great team of people to create some videos to walk you through the basic steps to what we'll be covering. We have a lot of videos up, and will continue to add more as people request them. **Visit www.bit.ly/npsocialmedia.** In the meantime, if you are not sure about something, that's what Google is for. Every question you have is answered somewhere on Google. Likely in the first result. Type in your question as you would ask it in plain English: "How do I copy and paste into Facebook?" And you will find videos or blog posts that answer your question.

That out of the way, let's get back to Linda.

Setting Up a Blog: A Primer

Linda had essentially two options for her blog: Either integrate the blog into the current website for the Historical Society or build it as a stand-alone site with links back to the main site.

Generally speaking, it's always preferable to have everything at a single URL, but if for budget reasons this isn't feasible for your nonprofit, don't sweat it. It's absolutely fine to have a blog on a different site. So if you have SmallvilleHistoricalSociety. org, you can also have SmallvilleHistoricalSocietyBlog.com or smallvillehistory.blogspot.com or whatever else you want to call it.

What are the pros and cons of either decision?

Having your blog on your site reduces confusion, so it's by far the best way to go. The downside is, if you don't already have a blog, it's *possible* that it could be expensive to create. And unfortunately, that's not a question I'm able to answer for you. It depends on who built your site and what "platform" they used to do it (like WordPress, or Drupal, or whether it's a custom platform specific to the web developer you hired). It's also possible that it could be added relatively cheaply. So you'll want to find out from your developer.

If it *is* outside of your budget to get a blog added to your site, then you'll have to have a separate blog. This leaves you, once again, with a decision:

- You can use a free blog service like Blogger.com that will cost you nothing out of the box.

- You can pay a little bit more to use a more advanced system that is built for consumers, which assumes you have a little working knowledge of how websites work (or are good at Googling questions that arise).

- You can pay a web developer to create your blog for you.

Here's what you might expect to pay for each of those options: If you pay a web developer, I estimate that you can get a nice-looking WordPress blog that matches the general look and feel of your site for $1,500 or less.

If you want to do it yourself, your hard costs probably won't be more than $175. You will need:

- A domain name (like SmallvilleHistoricalSocietyBlog.com, which should cost you less than $15).

- A place to host your site (I like Bluehost.com, which costs around $100 a year).

- A "content management system" or blogging "platform" to run the site (like WordPress, which is free).

- A template to make your site look good (you can find good templates at ThemeForest.net for less than $50).

For the totally free option, I recommend using Blogger.com, although it's still probably worthwhile to pay them $10 to $20 for the domain name. Smallvillehistory.blogspot.com is fine, but Smallvillehistoryblog.org is better, even if it points to the same place. There is one main benefit to using Blogger: Within just a few minutes, you can have your blog up and running.

Things to Include When Starting a Blog

No matter which route you choose, your blog should have these common elements:

- Your organization's logo

- A link to your organization's website (if it's a stand-alone blog)

- Links to your Facebook and Twitter accounts (when they are set up)

- A prominent place to collect email addresses (Constant Contact, Mailchimp, and other email newsletter services have HTML widgets that can be cut and pasted into the sidebar of your blog)

- An "about" page (which could be about the blog itself as much as it is about the nonprofit)

- A donate button (PayPal and other merchant services have HTML widgets that can be cut and pasted into your site)

- Google Analytics, or equivalent traffic measurement software

Linda's Blog

Linda tried to create her blog on her own using WordPress, but eventually decided it would take her too much time. She hired a local college student to customize a template for her and create the blog for $500 (she was glad to find some extra money in a technology budget she hadn't used yet). It took three or four weeks for it to be ready.

While the blog was being finished, she decided she would write some blog posts to have ready to go. She stared at an empty Word document and wondered ... just what exactly was she going to write about?

Writing Your Blog

Step one was to write a blog post. Oh, if it were only that easy! Blogging can be a little scary, especially if you don't consider yourself a writer. But even nonwriters can adapt to blogging relatively quickly. Here are some strategies to get you started that will help you launch a great blog.

Later, we will look at opportunities to use Facebook and Twitter to build a readership for the blog, but for now, we'll stick with the actual creation of blog posts.

A key principle of blogging to keep in mind is that you have two audiences for your blog's content (more on "content" in just a moment). The first is the immediate audience: your sphere of people who already follow you and want to read what you have to say. You are reaching out to them and giving them interesting or useful information.

The second audience is essentially an audience of one: Google. (Yes, some people use Bing and Yahoo. But what works for Google will work for them as well.) An excellent blog post can pay dividends for years to come as new people search for something ... and discover you!

What Is 'Content'?

A blog doesn't have to be just writing. A blog is a string of pieces of "content." What is content? Content is an easy catchall term for anything you put on the Internet: photos, status updates, PDFs, blog posts, YouTube videos, polls, e-books, tweets, and more.

Good content is what gets noticed and shared on Facebook. It's what persuades someone to sign up for your newsletter or to make a donation to your nonprofit.

Bad content distracts and confuses. Are your tweets poorly spelled, with links that don't work? Do you blog about topics that don't relate to your nonprofit's mission? Are your Facebook photos so small that people can't see them? Do they have watermarks from the stock photo service you stole them from?

And when you think of good content or bad content, it's a bigger question than just social media. It involves the rest of your website too. Does your website have out-of-date event information? Do you have a PDF of a job description online for a position you hired for more than two years ago? That is bad content.

This is not merely an aesthetic argument. *Each piece of bad content is an opportunity for a reader to get lost and miss the truly important information you really do want them to find.*

Why Should Anyone Read Your Blog?

As you get ready to start blogging, you'll need to answer this question early. If you are blogging because I told you blogging would be helpful to your nonprofit, that doesn't answer the question the *reader* is asking: Why should I read your blog?

Here are some questions to ask as you decide what your blog is about and why someone should read it:

- Can you provide useful information that will help people in their daily lives?

- Can you entertain them with funny stories about the hijinks that can happen behind the scenes of a musical?

- Can you help them remember that despite the bad news in the world, people are still doing uplifting and inspiring things?

- Can you, like the Smallville Historical Society, tell people about the back story behind the buildings and community they grew up in?

Get a handle on this question early.

Be Useful

Another way to think of the same question is to imagine what someone might type into Google to find a particular post on your blog.

They are probably not typing "Why is the Smallville Historical Society so awesome?" into Google. So Linda shouldn't spend all her posts telling them that.

Instead, maybe they are typing "Why does the Smallville bell tower lean?" Her blog can directly answer that person's question. She can provide helpful information. (In fact, if she is going to post about the bell tower, "Why does the Smallville bell tower lean?" is a great title phrase, because a number of people in Smallville are probably going to type exactly that phrase into Google.)

If they type "How do I extend my unemployment benefits in Maine?" and your nonprofit helps people find jobs in Maine, you are in a great place to help answer that person's question in plain English (or using a YouTube video that shows the step-by-step process) and dramatically affect that person's daily life.

In short, the common reason an organization starts a blog is to publish news and information about their organization. And it does that. But the best way it does that is by extending the work and mission of your nonprofit. If your nonprofit helps people in real life, then help them on the Internet too. If your nonprofit fosters civic discussion, then invite discussion online. If your nonprofit's mission is to entertain people with music or theater, then entertain them with music or theater (as copyright law allows) or lift up the curtain a bit and show the people how it's done.

Your blog is not just marketing. It is a new tool that will help you fulfill your mission for as long as the blog is online and people are using search engines to find information.

Figuring Out What to Post

Linda knew the general topic she wanted to cover and what she wanted to give readers: an understanding and appreciation of Smallville's pioneer history and how it affects life today. But she wasn't sure how to communicate that on a post-by-post basis.

She decided to do a quick brainstorm and get all her ideas on paper. Linda opened a Word document and started a list of post ideas. It eventually included scans of historical photos with descriptions, pictures of artifacts, event announcements, volunteer profiles, video interviews with actors in period costume, links to national news stories about historic preservation, profiles of historic buildings around Smallville, calls to donate as part of the annual campaign, "thank you" posts to donors and sponsors, and a lot more.

Looking over the list, she realized that if she ever did get around to writing all of these posts, a reader really would have the understanding and appreciation of Smallville history that Linda wanted to instill.

A blog is an unusual piece of writing: No individual post has to do everything you want the blog as a whole to do. But—

measured over time—those individual posts add up to a common message. Having a goal to aim for will help make sure that message is clear.

Linda sat back and looked at her list of ideas. Some she knew were duds the second after she wrote them. But she left them on the page anyway to inspire her later. The list would help trigger ideas when she wasn't sure what to post. And when the well ran dry, she could also dip into the photo bank or repost about an event coming up.

What follows are some other great ways to find ideas for blog posts.

Have a Calendar

I like looking for regular blog "features." It can be as simple as a "Wednesday Photo Day" where you always post a photo on Wednesday. A symphony could start each week with "Symphonic Monday" when it posts a YouTube video of a great piece of music.

Features make it easy on you as a blogger because you don't have to cast about looking for post ideas. Or at least you don't have to look as far. Hopefully, your regular feature has a wealth of things within the category, and all you have to do is find a good one for that week.

Write for Your Ideal Readers

As much as possible, write your blog post for a particular audience. Better yet, write it for a particular person. Imagine your ideal donor, your ideal volunteer, and your ideal event attendee (or whoever else makes sense for your nonprofit). Sketch out what they like, how old they are, what they're interested in. If it's not a real person, then name them. Give them a back story.

Let's say "Susan" is Linda's ideal donor. She's 55 years old, is considering early retirement from a cushy job, is a fourth-generation Smallville resident, and loves the town's history.

"Mark" is Linda's ideal volunteer. He's 65 years old, can make anyone laugh, and loves to dress up as a pioneer for kids. "Alison" is the ideal event attendee. She's 35, the decision-maker for a family of four, and always looking for family activities. These three fictional people are representative of Linda's ideal readers.

Now Linda can make sure that her blog posts target at least one of these people. If she's thinking about a post about a historical photo of pioneers, she can target that toward Susan, who loves learning more about the original settlers. Linda can write it conversationally, almost as if she were writing an email to Susan and telling the stories of the people in the photo.

Here's the real power of the idea: The next time Linda's looking for something to blog about, she can write a new blog post *about the same photo*, but this time in a way that would make Mark love it. Instead of telling the stories, she could write about the outfits of the people in the picture and give a short how-to guide for creating the outfit as a costume today.

Same photo, but by thinking about a different "ideal reader," Linda generates a whole new post.

What if Linda found an interesting story about a battle to save a historical bell tower in another state? If none of her three ideal readers would be interested in it, maybe it's not such a great topic for a post. Or maybe she just needs to put it into context so that Susan, Mark, or Alison *will* find it interesting.

Sketching out your ideal readers—even to the point of naming them—can have real power for building a useful blog and generating ideas for individual posts.

Read Blogs Similar to Your Own in Other Communities

Linda read blogs similar to hers from other museums and historical societies to generate ideas on what she could post. If another historical society posts about "The Five Key Moments in

Metropolis History," then that gives her a good idea: "The Five Key Moments in Smallville History" (or the six key moments, or however many there are).

Tie Your Story to Bigger Stories

This takes a little bit of creativity, but it can work well for creating timely and relevant blog posts. What is going on in your community *right now* that people are talking about? There's usually something big that seems to capture everyone's attention.

For example, a weather forecast says there's a heat wave coming to Smallville in three days and everyone's talking about where they'll go or what they'll do.

Linda could blog about how the early pioneers beat the heat in the days before air conditioning. A social service nonprofit could blog about how vulnerable homeless and low-income people are to heat waves. A community theater could offer a special "beat the heat" deal for its air-conditioned theater. An environmental advocacy group could suggest eco-friendly ways to enjoy the sun (like biodegradable water balloons or which lakes aren't having an algae bloom right now). A nonprofit dedicated to improving literacy could suggest great "beach reads."

Or let's say Google opens an office in downtown Smallville and announces it will hire 100 people. That would get a lot of people talking! Many nonprofits could find ways to blend their own stories with that big story. Linda could blog about how the new technology boom is like Smallville's railroad boom in the 1870s. A social service nonprofit could blog about how adding well-paying jobs could help boost important services. The Smallville symphony could suggest great composers and tracks available on Google Music. Maybe the environmental group could write about the transit options for new employees who want to commute without driving. And that educational literacy group could talk about the importance of reading in an online world.

There is one big trap to watch out for, however, and that is tying your message in with negative (or potentially negative) stories. One obvious reason is that you don't want to brand yourself with negative things (unless you are the solution to them).

Even then, tread very lightly. Stories about crime can often have a good tie-in to your organization. A social service agency could post about how a better safety net can reduce crime. Linda could post about famous Smallville criminals throughout history. But *should* they? Likely not. They'd be co-opting a tragic event for their own promotion. Not only is that tacky, but people will call you out for it. Suddenly *you're* the story.

Use Chapter Titles From Books About Your Topic

Pat Flynn from SmartPassiveIncome.com recommended an idea I really like for generating blog topics. Go to Amazon and search for books about your topic. Click on the "look inside" feature and find the table of contents.

Each chapter title is a possible inspiration for a blog post title! Here's an example:

Linda searched historic preservation and went through the table of contents for the first four books. Here are some of the chapter titles she saw:

- "The Preservation Movement in the United States"

- "Architectural Styles, Contextualism, and Design Guidelines"

- "The Legal Basis for Preservation"

- "Preservation Economics"

- "The Federal Preservation Program"

Linda jotted down notes and questions from these chapter titles and ended up with a short list of possible blog posts:

- "What was the first building in Smallville given a historic designation? Why?"

- "What is the architectural style of Smallville's historic buildings?"
- "Have there been legal battles over the historic status of a building in Smallville or a fight with a developer?"
- "How do historic buildings help the Smallville economy?"
- "Are there any buildings in Smallville that are on the federal register of historic buildings?"

Each of these questions was generated by looking at those chapter titles. And each could lead to one or more blog posts. Certainly, some of them might take a little bit of research, but Linda's experience with the Historical Society meant she knew a lot of the information off the top of her head and just needed confirmation of some specific dates.

For the topics Linda wasn't as familiar with, she made some notes and decided to follow up in her spare time over the coming months. Linda was personally interested in the topic, so it didn't feel like much of a chore. And as a side bonus, researching those topics was going to make her better at her job too.

How to Write Great Blog Posts

Now that you have a better idea of *what* to post, let's talk about how to post. What makes for a great blog post?

Tell Stories

Stories about individuals are better than just talking about a group of people. The specific can represent the whole. (There's a reason we're following the story of a woman named Linda in this book instead of just talking about social media and nonprofits in general.)

So profile volunteers, donors, staff, visitors, neighbors, customers, and more. What's their story? Why are they there?

What nice things do they have to say about you? What nice things do you have to say about them? And how does that relate to the bigger story you want to tell?

Refine Your Headline

A little sloppiness in a paragraph of your blog post is not ideal, but it's not the worst thing in the world. An unclear title for your post, though, is a kiss of death. Invest some extra time in your blog post titles.

Here are some ideas for writing eye-catching titles:

- *Write questions or phrases people might type into Google.* We saw this with the post title "Why does the Smallville bell tower lean?" It's clear and direct about what the post will contain and will likely get picked up by search engines.

- *Make a list.* Here are three reasons you will love lists (see what I'm doing here?): (1) Lists are usually easier to write, (2) they're easier for a reader to digest, and (3) they make better headlines. Framing a post as a list serves you and serves the reader. "Five key moments in Smallville history" is much stronger than "An overview of Smallville history" even if these two blog posts have pretty much the same content. Learn to love lists!

- *Write something provocative.* "Who is responsible for ruining the Smallville bell tower?" or "Why the Smallville bell tower will fall down by 2020."

- *Write something counterintuitive.* "Saved by the bell (tower)? How Smallville's leaning bell tower helps the local economy."

- *Mention someone famous or recognizable.* "An open letter to Mayor Smith about the bell tower." Or "Pictures of Pat Sajak and 8 other celebrities who posed in front of the

Smallville bell tower."

Always Use Photos

Photos tell stories just as well as blog posts. Visually, they also help break up text. A blog post almost always works better with an illustrative photo to accompany it.

If you don't have professional photos of your nonprofit, find a local photographer who might be willing to donate his or her time to give you a bank of photos that feature all the different services you offer. Ask the photographer to cover big events for you too.

Don't steal photos from a Google Image search. If you want "stock" photos, use a "creative commons" search on Flickr (flickr.com/creativecommons) to find free images, or buy them for a couple of dollars at istockphoto.com. Use a photo editor to shrink photos to an appropriate size (keep pixel size to about 500 or 600 pixels wide; keep file size under 200KB, if not under 100KB). If you don't have photo editing software, the online site pixlr.com allows you to make basic changes to photos, such as cropping and sizing.

Keep Blog Posts Short

There's no perfect length for a blog post, but unless you have a truly compelling story, I'd aim for 250 to 750 words (and only end up on the high end of that range if you're covering a single subject that wouldn't make sense to break up into multiple posts). Otherwise a photo, two paragraphs (100 to 250 words total), and a link makes for a good blog post.

The longer the piece, the better the writing—and the better the story—has to be to hold the interest of a reader.

Break Up Longer Pieces Visually

If you do have a longer blog post, then break it up, just as a magazine does. Use subheadings to define topic areas, break up long paragraphs into shorter ones, and—if your blogging software makes it easy—use pull quotes (quotations from the article highlighted in a larger font) to draw attention to important points. Basically, you're trying to make your post easy to skim for someone who just wants the big idea.

Spell-Check!

Proofread and spell-check! I hope that's clear enuf.

End a Blog Post With a Call to Action

If you targeted your post to one of your ideal readers, ask them to take an ideal action.

"If you would like the Historical Society to continue offering great programs like these, please <u>click here to make a donation</u>."

"Our costumed volunteers are the reason for our success. If you'd like to learn more about our volunteer opportunities, <u>please email us</u> and let us know!"

"Don't forget to <u>get your tickets</u> early to next weekend's Harvest Fest!"

Asking the reader for a donation, to volunteer, or to attend an event would fit for each of Linda's ideal donors. If none of these feel appropriate to the particular post, then you should end your post with a call to sign up for your newsletter. (Remember, that's why we're doing this.) It should be conversational. Here's a good example: "If you'd like to keep in touch with the Historical Society, please subscribe to our <u>e-newsletter.</u> It comes out once a month and we will never sell or give away your email address."

Other Tips on Blogging

As you start blogging, here are some big-picture questions

you'll want to consider as you get started.

Determine Your 'Voice'

If you ask a staff member to write a couple of posts while you are on vacation, you will want the blog posts to generally sound the same. It can be jarring for a reader to read dramatically different styles of posts, unless you call out the different authorship (more on that below). So it's important to know the "voice" of your nonprofit. Is it funny? Dramatic? Excited? Does it use emoticons and frequent exclamation points? (I hope not.)

If you're having trouble with this idea, reread your newsletters and official communications and you'll get a flavor of the style your nonprofit uses as its default "voice." Blog posts can usually be a little more casual than the official style, so it doesn't have to be identical, but it should be similar.

Write a few blog posts before actually publishing them to better understand what feels most comfortable to you and what you think will connect with your intended audience.

Who's the Author?

As part of the question of voice, it's worth deciding early whether you are writing with your name as a byline or if posts are labeled generically with no author. If you have your name on the byline of the post, and you are the executive director, you are essentially acting as the official voice of the nonprofit. Your blog post may use "I" as often as you use "we" because sometimes you are talking about yourself and sometimes the collective *we* of the nonprofit. Writing under your own name also probably gives you a little more license to make a joke and be a little less formal, since you're blogging as an actual person, not under the organization's name.

If you are blogging under the name of your nonprofit, you would probably exclusively use "we" as you write. This might make it a little easier to have multiple bloggers sound the same and to keep a standard voice on a blog. Without a doubt, you are the "official" voice of the nonprofit.

So given those two options, which do I recommend? In most situations, I like blogging under your own name better. First, it reinforces your name, which is good when you want to call up a donor. It gives you a little bit more latitude to stray from an official-sounding voice when you want to post something light or funny, because it is not an unsigned official statement with the organization as the byline. But if you need to sound official, you can easily change your tone and people shouldn't be thrown. If you want other bloggers to join you, they can post as themselves. (The very act of introducing themselves and what they do for the organization is a fine blog post.)

Blogging When It Feels as if No One's Reading

Sometimes you will post and no one will seem to notice. And you post again and then again, and you feel that you're wasting your time. Don't give up! In the next chapters we'll talk about building your audience using Facebook and Twitter. But until then, know that your posts are being indexed by search engines and that people who need the information in the post will eventually find it if it's relevant to them.

If, after following the suggestions in the next chapters, you still feel that no one is reading you, ask a disinterested eye to look at your blog and make recommendations. Is it physically hard to read (long paragraphs, no photos, bad spelling)? Are you using too much jargon (posts titled "How teachers can make sense of changes to RCW 69.51a" may not appeal to teachers if they don't know that RCW stands for Revised Code of Washington, or what 69.51a even refers to). Are you personally off-putting in your posts? OK, even a disinterested person might not tell you that, but sounding like a know-it-all, talking down to people, dismissing someone's ideas, and writing angry rants may not go over well.

If none of this describes you, then most likely the solution to feeling that no one is reading your blog is to keep writing, and to keep doing the social media work that builds an audience (again, next chapter).

How to Respond to Criticism (Real and Imagined)

Blog comments can be poisonous. Generally, I try not to read them, even on the best blogs with curated comments (*curating* comments means that someone manually approves which ones will be published).

You may choose to have comments enabled on your site. If you do, expect that there may be some negative feedback. It's part of being on social media. (Remember, the negativity likely would have happened even if you weren't on social media. You're just providing people a place where their negative comment can be heard and—hopefully—dealt with.)

So, if someone posts a negative comment about your blog post or your organization, you will be left with a decision: How do I respond to this criticism? Here are some ways to handle this:

- *You can delete it.* Unless you are a government organization, you have every right to delete something from your site, no matter how much someone cries "freedom of speech!" Freedom of speech means they can go get their own blog and write whatever they want to—*somewhere else.* There is no right for them to have their negative comments or slander on your own site.

- *You can ignore it.* There's a great saying on Internet forums and comment threads: Don't feed the trolls. What is a troll? Someone who is looking for a fight in an obnoxious way. Sometimes the best way to deal with a troll is to ignore them. (People who have genuine complaints or issues and are mostly respectful in addressing them are not trolls and should not be ignored.)

- **You can respond.** Even if you're dealing with a troll, a polite response can look good to everyone else reading the blog. Maybe you can't change the troll's mind, but your sincerity and effort to make things right will look good.

Which method you choose depends on what the comment says. If a comment contains foul language, bigotry, racism, or personal accusations, have no qualms about deleting it from your blog, or not approving it for posting. If you post about how great the next HarvestFest will be, and someone randomly comments about how badly the city maintains the roads where HarvestFest will be held and what are you going to do about it? ... maybe that's a comment worth ignoring. See if the commenter comes back, or if other commenters jump in about the roads.

But generally, I think most negative comments deserve a response.

Don't argue online. If they think your post is wrong, comment and apologize "if you got something wrong" and invite them to link to or email more accurate information. Maybe you did get something wrong. If so, correct the text and amend the original post with a statement that it has been updated. Don't just delete the error as if it never happened.

If someone is clearly angry about your organization or service, but it's not a post you feel is obnoxious or otherwise raises any red flag, then respond. Apologize if you disappointed them, tell them you'd love to address their concern, give your office phone and email address, and ask them to call so you can make it right.

Again, even if someone never reaches out to you (and they often won't, because one of the only reasons blog comments draw this kind of thing in the first place is that people can hide behind their anonymity), it will still look good to everyone else that you tried to make it right.

I want to write one caveat about deleting comments. It's almost always better to moderate comments before they are published than to delete them afterward. If you find yourself, for whatever reason, deleting comments regularly, then you should switch over to a moderated system where you approve comments before they go live.

Also, it is generally considered against the culture of Facebook to delete comments unless you have incredibly good reason to do so. Choose the highest possible bar for deleting a Facebook comment. Perhaps because people use their real name on Facebook, perhaps because it's seen as being different from blog comments … either way, it's considered bad form and can make more trouble for you later.

Don't Overly Self-Edit in Fear of Negative Comments

Emotionally, if someone leaves a negative comment that happens to really hit home, you'll have to deal with it however you best deal with conflict or disagreement. But be careful that it doesn't leave you feeling gun-shy. Sometimes after a negative comment, a writer can subconsciously avoid posting opinions, even tame ones, and their blog posts start to feel lifeless. If your post about how "historic preservation is good" got some negative comments, don't start writing posts about how "historic preservation is not bad, given certain conditions and qualifications so that no one can possibly disagree with this blog post." It's tempting to fall into that trap, but if you can avoid it, your blog will keep the tone and voice that made it enjoyable in the first place.

It's OK to Take a Break

Bloggers get tired. You told yourself that you'd post three times a week, but after a few months, it's started to slip to two. Don't punish yourself. All is not lost. I recommend giving yourself a goal: I will blog three times a week for three months. The timeline helps, because otherwise you might start to feel that you're never going to get a break. But committing for a specific length of time will give you a goal to shoot for and a natural time to stop and re-evaluate.

So if you feel you need a break, take a few weeks off when you hit your goal. Come back fresher and more rested. Look at any analytics data you've collected; compare your topic list to any new initiatives your nonprofit is thinking about undertaking; think about the kinds of posts you liked to write and focus on those; consider whether there's another member on staff who could contribute a post every couple of weeks to lighten the load.

Do another session of brainstorming ideas after that and hopefully you will have found a little more excitement to make the time you need to create a good blog.

In other words, it's better to take a break than to put up a lot of sullen posts that you clearly didn't want to write. Those won't do anyone any good—you or your readers.

Write a Guest Post on Another Blog

An excellent way to build readers for your blog is to write a guest post on another blog.

The ability for this to work for you depends on the kind and quality of blogs in your community or your subject area. But here's the general idea: Bloggers need posts, and you can provide one for them.

Despite all your brainstorming, after you've blogged for a few months, you will eventually find yourself staring at a blank page and having no idea what to post about. All bloggers find themselves in the same boat at one time or another. Blogging can be hard. A guest post can relieve the pressure.

Imagine that just when another blogger is trying to figure out what to post about, your email containing a sample 500-word blog post arrives in their inbox. They are *very* likely to use your guest post, and link back to your blog in the process.

The first step is identifying a blog you think is read by at least one of your "ideal readers." It should be locally focused, or in some other way show that a number of their readers could become your readers too.

Once you have found a few blogs you think could work, read at least a few weeks' worth of posts, and get a sense of the blog's style and what seems to get a lot of comments. Have there been guest blog posts before? If so, you're much more likely to be successful with this. Also, look for a sense of scale of the site. Is this a blog that people clearly read? If you're going to do this, you're going to want to reach as wide a group of readers as possible.

At this point, ask yourself if your nonprofit, and you as a blogger, have insight or information that you could offer readers of the blog you're targeting. So Linda at the Historical Society could write a post for an architecture blog (about historic preservation), a culinary blog (what did the pioneers eat?), or an environmental blog (how historical records from the pioneers show how Smallville's environment has changed), or even a theater blog (about costuming, "getting into character," etc.).

Then write! Keep it short. Since you're writing on spec and don't know if it will be published, you don't want to sink too much energy into this.

My recommendation is that you email and offer a guest blog post *with the post attached*. It's not too forward or presumptuous. You're showing the blogger right up front the quality of your writing, your expertise, and your ability to write for their audience. Send the email without a post attached, and you don't show the blogger any of that.

The great thing about this idea is that it wasn't wasted time. If that blogger isn't interested, you can make some slight edits and share the post on your own blog.

The Smallville History Blog

Linda's blog was up and running within four weeks.

She had drafted the first five posts to establish her voice, but she was enjoying it enough that by the time it was ready, she had written three more.

One was about the leaning Smallville bell tower, three were explanations of historical photos, two were event announcements, one was a feature on her longest-serving volunteer, and the last one was about a good historical walking tour down Smallville's Main Street.

Linda showed the posts to her staff and an old friend to get feedback, most of which were positive, although she heard from a few that her posts were too long. Linda edited the text down to make the writing tighter, and spaced the eight blog posts out over the course of three weeks.

She included a link to the blog in the next newsletter from the Historical Society and heard great responses to the first post about the Smallville bell tower, which had a lot of urban legends around why it leaned that she was able to clear up.

But now she was ready to start spreading the word elsewhere.

CHAPTER 3
Using Facebook Effectively

AS WE'VE DISCUSSED, with more than one billion users, Facebook is the essential social network you need to have a presence on. Having a Facebook page that is regularly updated with your photos, events, and news helps you keep in touch with donors, volunteers, and community friends.

Consider the alternatives: People screen their calls on the phone. Despite the importance of email, inboxes are getting overwhelming. Print mail is expensive. In short, it is increasingly hard to reach the people you want to reach.

But on Facebook … you are reaching people while they're taking a break at work, waiting for the bus, or trying to fall asleep. Your message is reaching them at a unique time: *when they are looking to be entertained and informed.*

Good thing we've worked so hard on blog posts that are compelling and entertaining to read!

Setting Up Facebook

Once Linda got her plans in order for the blog, she turned to Facebook to create a page for the Smallville Historical Society. Here are some basic things to look for as you create a page (or spruce up an existing page):

Set Up a Real Page

Or put another way: Follow the rules!

People have *profiles*. Businesses have *pages*. Facebook allows many profiles to be administrators of a single page. For example, Linda's personal Facebook profile and her bookkeeper's personal profile could both be admins of the Historical Society's page.

What they should not do is have a single login they share. Nor should they create a profile for the nonprofit with the first name Smallville and the last name HistoricalSociety.

I see businesses do this far too often because it seems easier, but I promise you it's a bad idea. First, you look bad to people who do know how Facebook works. Second, because it's against Facebook's rules, they can delete the account. That means all the work you put in is at risk of being erased.

The benefits of being a real "page" are high enough that it's worth a *slightly* more complicated setup.

Choose a URL

The default on Facebook is to use a long and gangly URL when you create your page. It's not ideal, and you should change it as soon as Facebook lets you (at the time of this writing you need at least 25 likes before you can change it). Change it when you can. A custom URL is an easier (and shorter) link to share with people outside of Facebook. It looks better too.

So choose a custom URL like Facebook.com/SmallvilleHistory. Choose wisely, and spell-check. Facebook may not let you change it later.

Make Your Logo Your Profile Picture

If that's not a great option (because you don't like your logo or don't have one), then use a picture of your building, service, or something else that is illustrative of what you do. As of this writing, Facebook has "cover photos," which is a great way to have a big picture that clearly shows off your nonprofit front and center on the site. If that changes by the time you read this, there will almost certainly be something similar. In other words, whenever Facebook gives you a chance to fill a blank space with a picture, take it.

Add All Your Information

Include your address, so people can "check in" when they come to your location. Add your website (both of them, if you have the blog and your normal website). Add your hours of operation. Add your mission, your founding date, and as much else as you can in the available fields.

Create an Album

People on Facebook love to look through photos. In fact, it's one of the main activities on Facebook. Put up an album of photos of a particular service you provide. Upload photos of a recent event (especially if they're good and not more than a year old). An arts organization might put up images of recent posters from its seasons. An environmental organization might put up pictures of the local watershed. Find *something* to post pictures of. Give people a reason to look through your site.

Be sure to add descriptive captions to your photos too. Why bother putting up photos if people aren't sure what they're looking at?

Like the Page

From your personal account, like the page. Invite your close friends to like it. Email your board members and send them the URL inviting them to like it if they're on Facebook. But don't send it out to your mailing list or donors just yet. Besides some pictures and basic information, there's not much there for them.

Sharing Blog Posts

Now that your page is live, it's time to start using it.

The most basic use of Facebook is to share your blog posts.

Write great posts, and then share them here.

When the blog post is live, copy and paste the link to the post as a Facebook status update with a one- or two-sentence note about it—maybe a quote from it or just a short explanation of why you thought it was interesting. Once you've added the link, Facebook should show you a preview of it below your text entry field. If you used a picture in your blog post (as you should have), it should show as a preview image on the Facebook status. At this point, you can delete the link itself from the field (since it will continue to show the preview below). And then post!

Keep Facebook open for a few hours to see if anyone comments or shares your post. Facebook commenters are generally much nicer than blog commenters (because they aren't anonymous) and they often comment more frequently (because it's easier to comment or just "like" a post than on a blog). Feel free to respond (positively, without getting into an argument) if you feel called to, or "like" people's comments.

Do this every time you post to your blog.

I don't recommend using automated services to post to Facebook or Twitter directly from your blog, or from Twitter to Facebook for that matter. Why? Because you have better judgment than a computer. Some posts benefit from a nice explanation on Facebook. Sometimes the formatting looks weird on the auto-post, but the computer doesn't know that. Sometimes a blog post is a short news item that would do better as its own Facebook update without a link back. You know best.

It takes a minute of extra work to post to Facebook and Twitter separately, but entering your posts by hand will be the cleanest for your readers.

Negative Responses

I don't think you will get that many critical comments or posts, but we need to keep coming back to it because how you handle it when they do happen is incredibly important. As I've said, social media is an opportunity for people who like your organization (or dislike you) to tell you how they feel, in public. Just like with blogging, you have to exercise judgment on how to respond to a negative comment, but your options are pretty much the same: delete it, ignore it, or respond to it. Again, with the exception of bigotry and other inappropriate language, the power of Facebook rewards responding professionally, courteously, and quickly to negative feedback. Your response will be seen by many, and how well you respond is often what people take away, even more than whatever the original complaint was.

If it feels weird to be giving complainers a place to publicly call you out, again keep in mind that they would have done it anyway. You just wouldn't have known about it. This way you are giving them a chance to feel heard and to fix the problem. If they'd just posted about a negative experience they had, and you weren't on Facebook, you never would have had the chance to address it.

What Else Can You Do With Facebook?

Not all of your Facebook posts should be links to your blog. You should be sharing a variety of different pieces of content: photos, events, links to other sites, and more. Here are some ideas that will help you create a lively Facebook page.

Promote Events

Facebook allows you to "create an event" on your page. This can be a powerful tool for getting people to come to your event. Bear in mind that people might click that they are attending an event but then not show up. If it's a ticketed or otherwise paid event, this can be tricky. So you may have to follow up with people who have said on Facebook that they'll come and remind them that they need to buy tickets if they haven't already.

In addition to creating events using Facebook's interface, you can also share an image of the invitation or a direct link to a registration page to promote the event on Facebook.

Post a Live Photo From the Event

Show off the crowd, your speaker, your volunteers, students ... or whatever else will look good on camera. Post it while actually at the event. Some people will say they were sorry to miss it; others afterward will tell you they enjoyed it.

Recap Events

Lots of opportunities here! Thank attendees, post sponsor logos, and—most importantly—post a variety of photos to an album of the event. After a successful event, do as many of these as are practical.

All in all, Facebook can help your event marketing *and* help you use your events to gain more attention for your nonprofit. I've read that in an age of social media, some people think events are almost more valuable for providing content for blogs and social media than they are for getting people together in the same room.

Focus on the Unique and the Interesting

Interesting things happen to us all the time. We win grants, we start a new year of classes, we have random encounters. Let me tell you, if a man in a full clown suit ever visited the pioneer cabin, Linda had better be ready to take his picture and post it on Facebook. "I'm not sure he understood what kind of costumes the pioneers wore ..." That would almost certainly get as many likes and shares as a post she'd spent an hour working on. One nonprofit here in Tacoma carved its logo into a pumpkin at Halloween, photographed it, and posted it on Facebook. That photo got more likes than anything they'd posted in months.

Or use Facebook to tell small stories that aren't big enough for a blog post. Like the one about the little girl Linda overheard asking her grandmother if she had ever traveled in a covered wagon.

Ask Questions

Since Facebook encourages actual communication with people who already like you, ask them questions. Not dumb things like "Coke or Pepsi?" but questions related to your mission.

"What plays would you like to see included in next year's season?"

"What advice would you give to someone taking their first drawing class?"

"What's your favorite old building in Smallville?"

"Do you know a breast cancer survivor who has inspired you?"

"Trying to figure out next month's training schedule. Do you prefer mornings or afternoons for education sessions?"

Don't commit to anything you can't later deliver, but don't ask meaningless questions. You have a whole group of people who like you ... ask them what they think about something and you just might find their answer to be helpful.

Post Links

Generally speaking, I think that when you find good links about things related to your mission, you should turn them into blog posts. But not every link is worthy enough to warrant a blog post, and sometimes you just may not have the time.

So don't worry about posting a link to another blog, a newspaper, or a YouTube video directly from Facebook. Just be sure to frame it: *Why* should readers care about this link? It doesn't have to be any longer than a sentence or two. But you always want to give context to a link or photo that you post.

Building an Audience on Facebook

As usual, the best way to get noticed anywhere is to have good content.

It's especially true on Facebook because when someone likes or comments on your status, other people see it, even if they haven't liked your page. So producing great blog posts, or posting great photos, will get you noticed.

All of the ideas above would help build interest, and therefore likes, on Facebook. But you need a core group of people to start that process going.

Here's how to get it started.

Invite People to 'Like' the Page

Once you've gotten at least one piece of content on the page, invite your personal Facebook friends (who are relevant geographically or in terms of their interests) to like the page. There's an option in the administration settings on the page in Facebook to do this.

Encourage People to "Check In" upon Arrival

You know how, before an event starts, the emcee will ask everyone to silence their cell phones? Forget that! Instead, ask people to check in on Facebook, Foursquare, Twitter, or whatever service they prefer, and maybe tag their friends while they're at it. If you're the emcee, get out your own smartphone and do it from the lectern. Seeing a few friends check in to an event on Facebook sends a strong signal to everyone not there that they are missing out.

Place a Widget on Your Website to 'Like' Your Page

Technically speaking, this might be the trickiest idea. There are ways for people to "like" your organization's *website*. But that's not what you want. You want an HTML widget on your website for people to like your Facebook page.

In Facebook settings, you'll be able to find how to create this widget. You should make it easy to find on your site. Sometimes it shows the profile pictures of people who like the page; other times it just shows a count of them. What you choose will depend on the size of the space you have for this feature. Once you've created the widget, then you can copy and paste it into an appropriate area on your website. *NOTE: I strongly recommend following an online tutorial for this if you attempt to do it yourself.* (I have one created at http://bit.ly/npsocialmedia, or use Google to find one.) Otherwise, ask your Web developer or a tech-savvy volunteer to do it.

If there's no good place for the whole widget on your site, you can generate a widget for something as small as just the "like" button or a Facebook icon to link to your page, and that should do it.

Notify Your Real-Life Fans About Your Facebook Page

It's absolutely appropriate to include your Facebook page URL in email communications to your volunteers, donors, board, and other key community members. But try to make it a little more substantive than writing, "On Facebook? So are we!" *Why* should someone follow you on Facebook? A short sentence is enough: "Follow along as we post historical photos and survey Smallville's historic buildings." Yes, maybe the reason you're giving is the same reason people should follow your blog. But a lot of people who wouldn't follow a blog have no problem seeing the same information on Facebook.

You can also put up signage around your facility (as appropriate). After you've let people know about the page, add the URL below your website address in your email signature.

Offer a Real-World Promotion

If you run a nonprofit that has customers or other patrons, you can experiment with a promotion for people who like your Facebook page (a 25% discount, a certain free item, etc.). This could also work well as a reward for people who check in (on Foursquare, Facebook, or any other location service) when they arrive, and then show you their phone to confirm.

Targeting Posts to Other Pages

This idea is similar to writing a guest blog post, but is focused on Facebook pages instead.

As you begin to use Facebook more, keep an eye out for other pages that are related to your page. For example, Linda might look for the state historical society page and pages for neighborhood and business groups near the pioneer cabin. She should take any opportunity she can find to post a link to their Facebook walls.

Imagine Linda writing a blog post about five great places to eat after going to the pioneer cabin. That post can be shared on the walls of five different restaurants. Each of those restaurants has a strong incentive to share that post with their audience— after all, they were just "featured" in your post. Will they all do it? Probably not. But that's OK. Even if only one or two out of five share it, you are getting new exposure to their followers on Facebook, many of whom probably didn't know there was a pioneer cabin near one of their favorite restaurants.

"The five most historic buildings in Smallville" can be shared on the walls of the neighborhoods those buildings are in, and on the walls of businesses in those buildings.

"A Historical Tour of Smallville" could be shared on the state historical society's Facebook wall, and on the wall of any stop on the tour.

If there is a page that you would *really* like to be featured on, then don't have any qualms about actually writing a post with them in mind. Think of them as a special ideal reader and tailor a post to that specific Facebook wall. I don't recommend doing this for *every* post—you don't want the tail wagging the dog too often. But getting your blog post shared by other organizations can be a powerful tool to getting noticed.

Different kinds of walls to target could include:

Regional, state, and national associations related to your nonprofit.

Local businesses, especially if they're sponsors of your nonprofit (i.e., thank them).

Geographic groups, like neighborhood business groups.

Tourism pages (especially for the arts and other attractions).

Interest pages. For example, 230,000 people like the Knitting Club on Facebook. What if you have a group of people who knit sweaters as part of a clothing drive? Could you profile them in a blog post and share the link on that Facebook page?

I hope the idea of writing a post specifically with the intent to share it on an organization's wall doesn't sound crass. The truth is, *any* social media strategy could be implemented poorly and in a way that turns people off. But if you introduce the link on the wall with positive comments or just a simple note ("Thought the Main Street Association would be interested in the Historical Society's blog post about Main Street's iconic leaning bell tower."), people won't see it negatively.

Pay for Facebook Ads

For surprisingly little money, you can pay to have your page show up on Facebook as a recommended page to like. A lot of customizable options are available. For example, if Jane likes the Smallville Historical Society's page, Facebook will show that page to her friends who live in Smallville. As more and more people in Smallville like the page, the friends of those people will see it. This strategy is effective even for $3 a day, although it's most effective at $5 to $10 a day. Turn it on for a month and watch what happens.

Maybe you want to attract people based on their particular interest. You can sort by that, too, and put your message in front of people who like reading, the environment, Harry Potter, or virtually any other interest people share. If you live in a large community, you can target not just by geography, but also by people who like certain things in that community (not to mention that you can also sort by age, gender, and education) for even more specific targeting.

Facebook also offers "sponsored" posts. Because of how Facebook organizes information, not everyone who "likes" your page will necessarily see every post you write. From a user's perspective, this is a good thing. If they log in six hours after your post, for example, Facebook will show them the posts of their closest friends above yours. From your perspective, it means that if you want as high a number of your followers as possible to see a post, you can pay Facebook for that privilege. Imagine that you had 1,000 people who liked your page, and you had an incredible piece of news you wanted to share with them. It's probably worth an extra $10 to make sure they all see it.

If you have the budget for it, I recommend spending $100 per month on ads for your page. If you can't afford to do that all year, then rather than shrink your monthly budget, I think you'll have more bang for your buck reducing the number of months, such as $100 in January, $100 in February, and then maybe nothing again until May and June. The snowball effect of this kind of advertising rewards showing the ads in larger bursts than as a small trickle over time.

About Your Own Facebook Profile

Do you use Facebook personally? If you followed the rules to create the Facebook page for your nonprofit, then you had to create a personal account first (it's necessary to log in from a personal account to create a new page). But the question is, how are you going to use that personal account?

It's totally fine if you just want to use Facebook to see your family's vacation pictures and update your nonprofit's page. But if you're willing, your personal Facebook account can be a powerful tool toward promoting your nonprofit.

Why You Should Be On Facebook

Why should you use your personal Facebook account, as well as a page for your nonprofit? Because everything in life is about relationships between *individuals*. When you ask someone for a donation, yes, she is giving to your nonprofit and its mission. But she is sitting down with you only because *you* have a good relationship with *her*.

In *The Little Book of Gold*, I talk about how to throw a breakfast fundraiser and how it is all about relationships. You ask people you have relationships with to be table captains, and the table captains ask people they have relationships with to attend.

The benefit of Facebook is that people will get to know you *as a person*. Even if you're just posting pictures of sunsets and cats. When they run into you in real life, they will know your name, they will likely know where you work, and they will remember that last week you posted a picture of the delicious-looking pretzels you baked from scratch. And you will likely remember their name, their place of work, and their vacation photos from Cancun.

These are all fairly shallow things. We're not talking about deep friendships, necessarily.

But what more do you need to strike up a real conversation with someone in real life? In a pre-Facebook world, you would spend your first few minutes with someone talking about the weather and going through small talk before any real conversation could happen. But now ... *all that's already happened*. When you meet someone you've been friends with online, but haven't met in person or haven't seen in a while, you can connect more quickly. You already know something about them and what they've been up to. Where's your common ground? Connect! As two *real* people.

I am friends with someone on Facebook who one day announced that she had published a book. I hadn't met her in person, but I happened to see her that very night walking in the park. I knew what she looked like, and she knew what I looked like, so it was easy to say hello and congratulate her.

We started talking about writing and publishing and we eventually met for coffee. We now have an actual relationship. Not a close one, certainly, but it's a real connection. And if we hadn't been on Facebook, I would have passed her in the park without a second thought, without making a new connection. If she hadn't posted about her book, she wouldn't have had the wonderful experience of someone stopping her in the park on her launch day and congratulating her (and let me tell you, that's pretty much the dream for a writer). She shared a little of herself online and reaped the benefits.

A personal Facebook account is essential to building relationships in the community.

Finding Friends

Just as when she created the page for the Historical Society, Linda put a little more work into her own Facebook profile. She uploaded a professional picture as her profile image and also filled out her hometown, her birthday (she left off the year, which is always an option), and her job title. Then she started "friending" people. Yes, that's a verb now.

Linda friended her volunteers that had Facebook accounts and some key donors she genuinely liked. She also added the executive directors of other local nonprofits around Smallville and some of the owners and managers of local businesses that she knew from her work. After she started adding friends, Facebook started suggesting more people she might know, and Linda was surprised how many names she did indeed know. There were also a lot of names she recognized, but didn't know personally.

But should she friend them on Facebook if she didn't know them? Facebook certainly wanted her to.

She decided to hold off … for now.

This is entirely up to you. I have no problem friending someone I barely know, as long as they are in my local community. Some wait until they meet in person before sending an invitation. Others send a Facebook message to a new person first as a friendly greeting, suggesting why they feel they should connect. I don't know that there is a right way. But there's no reason you can't take it slow and decide.

You will find very soon that people will start friending you that you don't know, and you have to face the same question: Should you accept if you don't know who they are?

I'm encouraging you to have an active personal Facebook account because I think it will be helpful to your nonprofit. So my recommendation is that if someone you don't know asks to friend you—and they are in your community or otherwise could be interested in your nonprofit—accept the friend request.

After a week or so, Linda had built up from 80 friends (mostly old school friends and family) to 250 by adding people in her professional spheres in her community. But she wasn't quite sure what to do with them all now. Her Facebook feed was filled with things she didn't care about. And she wasn't sure how this was supposed to help the Historical Society.

Tips for Making Facebook Easier

Not everyone necessarily has to *like* Facebook to use it. You may find it difficult to manage, that your privacy settings seem to change willy-nilly every time Facebook updates its settings, or a host of other complaints familiar to any longtime Facebook user.

But there are some tools and ideas that will make using Facebook more enjoyable and more effective for you.

Hiding People and Activities

Over time, Facebook will automatically begin sorting what information you see in your feed based on your activity. But if there's someone who posts things that upset you, annoy you, or otherwise ruin your day, then you should hide them.

Facebook makes this easy to do with a single click. Do you have a friend who posts about every cow they bought on Farmville? You can choose to hide any post by that person, or all posts about Farmville, no matter who's playing it. I've hidden people when they post very frequently and I don't know them very well. And I've hidden a bunch of games, horoscopes, and other apps that I'm not interested in seeing.

(And, for the record, no one can tell that you've hidden them, so do so freely.)

Organize Your Friends

If you're just getting started on Facebook, you might find it helpful to create lists of people early: let's say "close friends and family," "old friends," "Smallville," and "everyone else." The point is that you can post things that are personal and only relevant to your close circle without everyone knowing too many details.

Lists aren't foolproof! I assume that if I put something on the Internet, even if it's only for a certain audience, everyone might end up seeing it. I'm always mindful of that central truth. But you should generally feel OK about using lists for keeping family photos or other personal news *mostly* private.

Instead of thinking about it in terms of privacy, though, it's probably more helpful to think about it in terms of relevance. What would this list of people care about? Does your list of Smallville friends care about your out-of-state family reunion? Do your out-of-state relatives care about your nonprofit's news? Likely not. So when you post about one topic, share it only with the list, or lists, that would most care.

Just as earlier we talked about hiding people who posted things that were irrelevant to you, organizing friends by list helps you make sure that you don't post things that are irrelevant to someone else—and thus, get hidden yourself.

But don't silo *everything*. One of the great things about using Facebook is that people can see you are a real human being outside of work. You have a family, you have hobbies, you read books and watch movies, you take time off to go on road trips. The people you work with as colleagues, donors, patrons, or volunteers will enjoy learning a little more about you as a person.

"Like" Other People's Cat Photos

If you see something you like—cat photos, baby photos, a funny status update—click the like button. "Like" a few photos of someone's favorite pet and they're much more likely to pay attention to your own status updates. It's also an excellent way for people you don't know very well to see your name.

I hope this advice doesn't sound crass.

I'm *not* saying you should indiscriminately "like" things you don't actually like. Facebook is a place to be a real person. All you're doing is communicating what you like with a simple click. It feels good for the person whose update you liked, and you are beginning the initial steps of forming online relationships.

Post Your Own Photos and Updates

Everyone's comfort level with this is different. *And, to be clear, at no point am I suggesting that you should share more than you are comfortable with.* When it comes to protecting your own sense of privacy, there is no wrong way to approach this. If you don't want to put pictures of your family on Facebook, then don't. It's as simple as that.

But at the same time, you should be sharing *something* about yourself. What do you talk about when you meet someone new? What sort of small talk do you make? Do you like movies? Do you like dogs? Running? Knitting? Camping? Reading? Baking?

How about something more specific ... Do you have an orchard and like to graft limbs from pear trees onto apple trees? Do you play board games from the 1960s? Have you watched every single *Dr. Who* episode? These are not topics that are controversial or overly personal. But they are part of who you are, and if you feel comfortable sharing them, then I encourage you to do so.

Don't go crazy with it. If you write a 500-word summary of every *Dr. Who* episode and share five summaries a day, you're going to get hidden from people's timelines. But if you love baking homemade pretzels, post a picture of a good-looking batch. Mention that you're excited for the new season of *Dr. Who*. Post about your marathon training.

Post pictures of sunsets, sunrises, rainbows, and first snowfalls. Complain about the weather. Be appreciative for sunny days and cool evenings. Recommend a good mystery you just read. Share an inspiring article, even if it's not related to your work.

Facebook is, in many ways, online small talk. Participate, to whatever degree you're comfortable with.

Caveat: Discuss Politics and Religion at Your Own Risk

You have a few choices when it comes to controversial topics. In order of least controversial to most controversial, the first choice is to ignore every controversial topic and keep your Facebook wall focused on sunshine and roses. The second is to share your views about controversial topics with a select list, like your close friends and family list (always bearing in mind that you are still posting something on the Internet and that once you do there's no 100% way to guarantee something stays private to a certain group). The third choice is to just assume that everyone is an adult, and if they don't like your post about your feelings about Barack Obama, they can deal with it.

But just as when you talk about these things in real life with a group of people who aren't all close friends and fellow believers, these kinds of topics can incite very strong feelings in others and catch you off guard. When you post about them on Facebook as opposed to mentioning them in conversation, whole arguments can spring up around them that never would have happened at a restaurant. Imagine posting a link right before bedtime to an article about abortion … and waking in the morning to discover that over the course of 22 comments your best donor and your sister—who live in different states and don't know each other—are in a huge argument over the question of whether life begins at conception.

That kind of situation is a worst-case scenario (although *not at all* out of the realm of what can happen on Facebook). If you say something that upsets someone, they'll probably ignore it. Or, if it's really upsetting to them, most likely they'll hide you in their stream (you'll never notice) or unfriend you (you'd notice only if you went searching for them again and saw that you weren't friends anymore). Maybe it's not the worst thing in the world, but if that person who hid you or unfriended you was a donor, then what was the point of friending them on Facebook in the first place?

If your relationship with your church, your position on abortion, or your identification as a Republican or a Democrat is central to who you are, then I'm not going to tell you to avoid putting any of it on Facebook. You won't get anything out of Facebook if you're not sharing something of who you are, and if this is it, then by all means, share.

But if your reasons for using Facebook are largely professional, then my strong recommendation would be to share these kinds of topics with a list of people that comprises friends and family, and keep your professional contacts out of it.

Share Your Work

Every so often, when you have a really good blog post, or a really good event coming up, share from your personal account a status update from your organization's page. Don't do it every time—you'll be double-hitting people who have liked the organization's page and are also friends with you. But you should do it when you have something good, and suggest that people like your organization's page to keep up with more.

Sometimes you don't even need to use the "share" feature. It's appropriate, and often a good idea, to say in your own status update that you are excited about an upcoming event or a new program.

Be the Spokesperson for Your Organization

As the executive director, you are a spokesperson for your nonprofit. Your personal Facebook page is a good place to step into that role. You are representing your nonprofit to other executive directors, community leaders, and businesspeople. You want the general public to like your organization's Facebook page. But from your personal page you want yourself to be noticed on the Facebook walls of other leaders in your community. This is about networking and branding more than it is about trying to friend everyone who might like your organization.

If your nonprofit has a certain position on an issue in the community, consider advocating for that position from your personal account—as long as you do so respectfully and with the understanding that people who have an opposing view are on Facebook as well.

If there's news—good or bad—about your organization, you can write it up and share. Here's an example:

"Some sad news from the Historical Society. Despite all our precautions, a cash register was stolen early this morning from the pioneer cabin. No money was taken, but there was some light damage from the break-in. After a lot of consideration, we've decided to get an alarm service. Any good local recommendations for a company who could take on a unique project like a 150-year-old cabin?"

This is the kind of post that everyone who likes the Historical Society doesn't necessarily need to see. But the executive director, who is asking for recommendations from her professional and community contacts, could easily post it. And notice, it's *helpful* to you too. If you had no idea which alarm or security company is the best in town, a post like this will get you a short list to start from with good recommendations and stories.

Don't Play Games

A lot of people play Farmville and Bejeweled and all sorts of social games on Facebook. My recommendation is to skip them. Play games elsewhere. Don't have a service automatically post a horoscope to your feed. You don't want to give someone a reason to hide you. Yes, they can hide just the games. But people may hide you accidentally in the process. Don't give them the excuse.

The Smallville Historical Society on Facebook

Linda was able to get the Historical Society from 10 likes to

60 likes in a week. After that, it seemed that the rate of growth was slower—only a couple per week—but that it would spike if a particular photo or blog post got a lot of likes or comments. Eventually she tried a month of Facebook ads for $100 and saw her likes jump to 400.

Some of the museums in town had more than a thousand likes on Facebook, but they'd been on it a lot longer too. As long as Linda saw at least *some* growth, she would be happy with it.

CHAPTER 4
Using Twitter Effectively

TWITTER IS A global online town hall. It is great for broadcasting news, consuming news, and talking about something happening right *now*. It has many similarities to Facebook, but the two services differ in several key ways:

- Twitter has a 140-character limit for posting—its defining characteristic.

- Twitter is—by far—the quickest place for news to spread. Much faster than Facebook.

- Twitter does not have any expectations of having a "real name" tied to an account. It's entirely appropriate and encouraged to have an official account for your nonprofit.

- There is no mutual acceptance of "friendship" as on Facebook. If you want to follow someone's updates, you click "follow," and you're in. (The exception is protected accounts, but your account should be public and most of the people you will be following will probably have public accounts as well.)

Setting Up Your Twitter Account

Here are the important things you'll want to get right as you set up your Twitter account.

Choose a Username and a Real Name

Unlike Facebook, Twitter allows you to change your username (or "handle") later. But it has to be less than 15 characters long, which can introduce some challenges if your name is longer than that. The Smallville Historical Society is 27 characters long, which meant that Linda had to find a way to express the same idea in about half the characters. You may find similar issues.

Try to go for description and simplicity rather than shortened and illegible words. SmallvilleHis (13 characters) is mostly readable, but leaves out the key word. Smallhistory (12 characters) might be better. SmallvilleHS (12 characters) could be Smallville High School just as easily as Smallville Historical Society.

SVHistory (9 characters) might be my favorite of Linda's options because it abbreviates the part that is most understood (to someone in Smallville) and keeps the focus on the organization's mission—history. I live in Tacoma and anyone locally would understand abbreviations like Tac or TTown. So TacHistory would be readily understood by more people than TacomaHis, which leaves a lot more room for confusion. You'll know what's most appropriate for your own community if you have to figure out a shortened version of your own name.

Choose Your Picture

I recommend using the same profile picture you used on Facebook as your Twitter profile picture. If you used your logo, choose your logo. If you used something else, use that. I like keeping the same profile picture for a nonprofit between social media services. If you change your page's picture on Facebook, remember to change it here too.

Choose Your Design

Twitter allows for a fair amount of customization. You can make your Twitter page have your nonprofit's colors, and you have the option of uploading two pictures: a header image and a background image.

Background Twitter images can look really great or really terrible. Maybe you have a great shot of your nonprofit, but when you upload it, it's mostly behind the main part of the website, and people only see a tiny fraction of it. The Twitter background images that work best are usually narrow and vertical, so that they fit entirely on the left sidebar. If you don't have something that works, just use one of the stock options from Twitter.

(I do recommend switching from the default, though. What we're trying to do is make sure your account page looks like it wasn't just opened and then forgotten.)

For a header image, find something simple and clean, since it will be displayed behind text on your page.

Describe Your Nonprofit in 140 Characters or Less

This can be a little tricky, but think of it as good practice for future tweets, which have the same character limit. Your description should be as concise as possible, with no wasted words. Write and rewrite this until it's packed with information.

The Smallville Historical Society preserves Smallville's history through educational programs and its historic pioneer cabin. (116 characters)

This sentence fits, but Linda would be wasting an opportunity if she went with it. There's a lot more that can be fit into 140 characters. She kept revising.

The Smallville Historical Society preserves our community's history at the pioneer cabin and thru school programs. Great for families! (134 characters)

Already more detail.

We are dedicated to preserving Smallville's history. Step back in time at the pioneer cabin (at Elm and 3rd) and find out what life was like in the 1860s. (153 characters)

This was Linda's favorite so far, but it went too long. She saved a lot of characters by removing "The Smallville Historical Society" and replacing it with "we." Since the name of the organization can be in the title, this may not be needed here. A few edits can get it down to 140 characters, though.

We are dedicated to preserving Smallville's history. Step back in time to the 1860s at the pioneer cabin (at Elm & 3rd). Great for families! (140 characters)

Exactly at the limit. Linda was able to squeeze in the mission, the cabin's location, and a plug for families. Not bad for 140 characters. But it took her 10 minutes of revising to get it there. It's time well spent.

Choose a Website

You get only one field where you can add your website, so if your blog is separate from your website, you'll have to choose. Since one of the main reasons you're on Twitter at this point is to share blog posts, I'd choose the blog.

Enter Your First Tweet

Choose something simple, preferably not: "Trying to figure out this crazy #Twitter thing. LOL." How about: "The Smallville Historical Society is excited to join Twitter! Who should we follow?"

Follow Your Local Newspaper

We'll talk about building up an audience and followers later, but for now, search for your local newspaper (if you have one) and follow its Twitter account. Don't follow too many more people just yet. When you follow someone, it will notify the person that you're following them, and—as on Facebook—if they click over to see what you're about, they won't find too much there yet and may be less likely to follow you back.

What to Tweet

Many of the same things that Facebook can be used for are equally effective on Twitter, but condensed to 140 characters.

Share Blog Posts

As with Facebook, the most basic use of Twitter is to share your blog posts. You don't need as full an explanation of the post, though. *New Blog Post! "Why the Smallville bell tower will fall down before 2020"* is a perfectly fine tweet. To make sure your tweet is under the 140 character limit, copy and paste the link first. Twitter will use its automatic URL shortener and will show you how many characters you have remaining to write your "headline."

Promote Events

Tweet links to event pages on your website. Be sure to have a date or day in the tweet. Don't force people to click through to find out the key information.

Post a Live Photo From the Event

Show off the crowd, your speaker, your volunteers, students … or whatever else will look good on camera. Tweet it while actually at the event.

Live-Tweet an Event

This is one of those activities better suited to Twitter than Facebook. Live-tweeting an event is like covering it as a journalist. You are selecting 140-character-sized bits of information and posting them rapidly for people who couldn't attend. If you have a speaker, you would choose short quotes or general statements from their speech to tweet. If someone were following along, they would get a very good idea of what the speaker said, just not the word-for-word version of it.

Summarize the key points of a presentation, quote a couple of jokes, and maybe even solicit questions for a speaker from Twitter.

If the audience is big enough, you might find that other people in the audience are also tweeting about it. You can prepare in advance and encourage this by publishing a hashtag for anyone who wants to live-tweet an event with you. For example, the Smallville Historical Society's annual breakfast fundraiser might have a local architect speak who specializes in historic preservation. You could go with a hashtag like #SVHist or #HistBfast. The goal is to have something very short that people can attach to the end of their tweets about the breakfast. Since everyone will have the same reference point in their tweet, anyone—whether they are at the breakfast or not—can search Twitter for it and see what people are saying about the breakfast. You can keep track of what people are saying, and so can those who weren't able to make it.

When people tweet good things about the speaker, you can retweet them to your own audience, showing how well your program has been received and further reinforcing to people who aren't there that they should try to make it to your next event.

If you will be too busy at the event to live-tweet it yourself, find a volunteer who readily understands Twitter and what live-tweeting is, and give them the username and password. This takes a lot of trust, so it should be someone who has experience with this or who somehow demonstrates to you they have the judgment to not start swearing or inserting their own opinions.

Retweet Relevant News

You should follow major organizations in your specific industry and accounts that regularly tweet news about it. When something is relevant to your audience, retweet the news. Your audience will appreciate the information. If you use a third party app for Twitter on your smartphone, you can often choose to "quote" a tweet, which will allow you to add a few words of context in front of a tweet.

Reply to People

You should usually reply to tweets that mention you, even if it's just to say, "Thanks for the mention!" But if you see people who need help or have questions, and you know the answer—*and are on brand*—go ahead and reply to them and help them out.

What does it mean to be "on brand?"

Well, if someone asked for help on electrical wiring it might look odd if the Historical Society were providing the answer. Unless it was a question about wiring in historic buildings.

Context matters. Replying to people and answering their questions or providing helpful information is what Twitter is all about. But be sure it's grounded in the organization and its mission. If you personally have expertise in bread baking and want to reply to someone who is looking for help, but it makes no sense to come from your nonprofit's account, then maybe it's time to open up a personal Twitter account.

It's always appropriate to give kudos and thanks to fellow organizations in your community. The Historical Society *should* congratulate the art museum on its big new grant. It's a small way of celebrating the successes of similar organizations, and makes them more likely to help you celebrate your own successes.

Ask for Action

It's totally fine, and can be helpful, to ask people to retweet your tweet. Don't do it every time, but if you have a big piece of news or something exciting to share, especially something time-sensitive, then go ahead and put a "Please RT!" on the end of your tweet. And thank those who retweet you afterward.

Every so often, you can also make a direct call to action to give, volunteer, attend an event, or sign up for your nonprofits' newsletter. Don't turn your Twitter stream into a nonstop sales pitch, but it's OK to drop these in every so often.

Know Your Twitter Vernacular

Pay attention to other people's tweets, especially when you see abbreviations and acronyms. If you see something you aren't familiar with, Google it. "What does MT on Twitter mean?" will yield plenty of helpful results. (It means "modified tweet," which indicates you are retweeting someone but you changed their tweet slightly, without affecting meaning, to make it fit into 140 characters.)

Participate in Twitter trends when they are appropriate. Every Friday, for example, users suggest good accounts to follow, called Follow Friday. They use a hashtag like #FollowFriday or just #ff and list a few accounts they recommend. If there are people in your field who have great tweets, or a few accounts that are themed (like neighboring businesses), then you can list a couple of them in the same tweet.

The main point is to be active on Twitter and still provide helpful information to your followers.

Avoid Automated Services (for now)

For a variety of reasons, I don't recommend using a service to automatically tweet Facebook updates or send tweets to Facebook. The format is just too different. Either all of your Facebook posts will be tweet length, when they could have been longer. Or your posts will be cut off mid-word (to fit Twitter) and people will have to click through to understand what you're trying to say (if they bother at all).

In addition, I would avoid services that allow you to preschedule tweets. It might sound appealing to post tweets at the beginning of the day and then not worry about it, but I just don't see this being worthwhile for the volume of tweets you probably will have. (Not to mention that if there is a huge news-making event that happens at 4 p.m. that everyone is tweeting about, your prescheduled tweet from that morning is going to get either ignored or mocked.)

Other services let you automatically take actions when certain things happen: someone follows you so you automatically send them a direct message thanking them. Again, I think it's worth avoiding these services, as they can feel like spam to your new follower.

Building an Audience on Twitter

Remember how we spent all that time making a really succinct description in your Twitter account? This is where it's going to start paying off. Whenever anyone visits your Twitter page, they are going to judge whether they want to follow you based pretty much on two things: what your description says and what your last few tweets say. You can boost people's willingness to follow by having a good profile picture and a good background image, but generally, people want to know who you are and what you have to say.

But how do you get people to even notice you? The blog post links you've tweeted and your participation on Twitter will start to get noticed, albeit slowly. You can jump-start this process with a targeted effort.

Start Following People

The best way to get people to follow you on Twitter is to follow them. They will get a notification that someone has followed them, and if your username and description are interesting and relevant to them, they'll probably follow back.

So, who to follow?

- Organizations similar to yours in your community, neighboring communities, and elsewhere, if they have a good Twitter feed (you can learn something from them).

- News organizations in your community. Look for TV, print, and online media, including bloggers.

- Government accounts, such as an official account for your city or county government.

- Neighboring businesses.

- Your Facebook friends or email contacts that are on Twitter. This can yield good results of people you should follow, although I don't recommend doing a mass-follow, where you follow everyone whose email address you have. Look for those who are appropriate to the nonprofit or in your local community and follow only them.

- Donors, foundations, and volunteers. Some may not have gotten picked up in your contact search for whatever reason. Search for names of your top donors and common volunteers.

- High-volume tweeters in your community. Do a search for the name of your city and then narrow it to people who mention it in their profile page (at the time of writing this, it's called searching for people instead of searching tweets, and it will search usernames and descriptions for keywords). It's an excellent way to find people in your community who have a lot of followers already (and thus can spread the word about you effectively later).

- Local politicians and candidates for office. They all have incentive to follow nonprofits that are doing good work in their community.

By this point, you will have followed a fair number of people. And hopefully, a number of them will have followed you back. (It might be useful later to add them to lists as you follow them. So Linda might create a "Smallville" list for anyone she follows in Smallville, a list of "History and Preservation" for anyone related to the field, and maybe one more for "Neighbors and

Volunteers" where she can file people she wants to keep in touch with more frequently.)

Give it a rest for a day and come back and see who's followed you. When you do, Twitter will also recommend people for you to start following. Sometimes these are paid promotions, sometimes they're celebrities, but sometimes they're other local people that you may not have found otherwise. They're compiled by looking at who you follow and making educated guesses about who else is similar or popular. Keep an eye on it, or check out the "view all" option and look for more people in your community and your field that you missed on the first pass.

Now, Really Start Following People

Want to take this to the next level?

After you've built up a few tweets and have a hundred or so followers, you can start getting really targeted. *Start following some of the people who follow other organizations like yours.*

For example, people who follow the Smallville Art Museum are a likely demographic of people to follow the Smallville Historical Society. Go to the museum's Twitter page and view their followers. You'll be able to see information on each one and decide if they make sense for you to follow. Look for one or two key traits such as location and interests as you make up your mind. Keep in mind, the main reason you are following them is to generate the notification and put your information in front of them.

The consequences of following an individual who is not an ideal match for your nonprofit is close to zero. That said, if you follow 2,000 people in an hour, Twitter will probably suspend your account as being a spam account. So find an appropriate balance. An easy way to do it is to choose one account a day that you'd like to target, and sort through their followers. Do that for a week (it shouldn't take more than 15 minutes a day) and you'll really start to build up an audience.

As usual, sort those new follows into lists as well. At the very least, this will help you remember later why you followed them in the first place.

Paddling Up the Twitter Stream Successfully

By this point, you might be following several hundred accounts. Which means that most likely you are going to be receiving several tweets per minute during the day.

Unlike your personal Facebook, where you probably know most of the people you are friends with, on Twitter you probably won't. Which means their tweets will be largely meaningless to you and you might be tempted to give up on the whole thing.

Resist that urge!

Here are some easy ways to handle having a large stream of tweets coming at you.

- **Don't try to read everything.** A Twitter stream is meant to be dipped in and out of when you have time. Don't try to read every tweet since the last time you checked Twitter. It'll take way too much time.

- **Use lists instead.** If you want to keep closer tabs on the accounts that aren't strangers to you, put them in a list and check it more regularly. It's a good way to make sure that you see tweets from neighboring businesses or regional associations that you are much more likely to want to respond to and retweet. Sometimes some of those accounts you don't recognize will still reply to you and retweet you. Even if you don't know who they are, they clearly like you and are spreading the word about you. It might be a good idea to add them to the same list as the other accounts, so you can look for more opportunities to interact with them. (If you do, make sure the list is generically titled to be inclusive, since people can see where they are listed.)

- **Smartphones make Twitter easier.** I usually prefer

reading tweets from my phone rather than from the desktop. I like that I can check in for a few minutes in those random bits of downtime. You can use the official Twitter app, or use one of several good options like Tweetbot or Twitterific.

- ***Get notifications about replies.*** If you have a smartphone, you can set it so that you get notifications about replies and retweets. You can also set Twitter to send text messages or emails about the same thing. Go with whatever you're most comfortable with, and with whatever you feel least disrupts your life outside of work. Whichever you choose, it's really helpful to see when your handle is mentioned so you can reply within a few minutes or hours instead of whenever you happen to next check Twitter.

- ***Plan a time to check Twitter.*** It's not a bad idea to set a time to check Twitter. A few minutes—15 minutes tops—and you'll see if there's anything from the day that's worth retweeting or replying to. If you're enjoying yourself, set a common time twice a day.

- ***Don't be afraid to unfollow someone.*** If you find someone in your feed who was clearly not a good choice to follow, you may want to consider unfollowing them. Maybe they moved; maybe they never followed you back (a good sign they aren't interested in you). In those cases, go ahead and click unfollow. Also, you'll want to remove them from any lists you put them in.

- ***A few months in, do a "mass unfollow."*** A couple of months after starting your account, you might want to cull the list of people you follow. By this point, you've given people ample time to follow you back. Some of them may not use their accounts; some of them just might not care about your message. One way to do this is to go to the website friendorfollow.com and sort your followers by whether they follow you or not. Very likely there are some accounts listed that you followed because you thought they might be interested in you (as opposed to your being interested in them). If they still haven't followed you, feel free to unfollow them, with no consequences. You might want to do this especially if the list of people you follow is significantly higher than the number of followers you have.

A Word on Managing Two Accounts

If you start to enjoy Twitter and are interested in opening your own account, you'll encounter a common issue for anyone who manages more than one social media account: keeping them straight. How best to make sure that you don't post personal tweets to your nonprofit's stream?

First, don't sweat it. It will very likely happen, and it happens to the best of us.

A tweet showed up on the official Red Cross Twitter account in 2011, talking about buying "Dogfish Head's Midas Touch" beer—with the hashtag #gettnglizzerd, no less. This was clearly the work of someone who meant to post to their personal account, and not the Red Cross.

People had a great time on Twitter poking fun at them. But the Red Cross didn't panic. They posted a joking tweet: "We've deleted the rogue tweet but rest assured the Red Cross is sober and we've confiscated the keys." I'm not sure they had to delete the rogue tweet, but it was a pitch-perfect response.

In addition, Dogfish Head Brewery posted about it and encouraged people to give money to the Red Cross as well.

There are pieces of software that help you manage your Twitter accounts, but if you are worried about this, I recommend keeping things separate. Using separate browsers and separate apps is one way to do so. If you use Chrome as your main browser on your computer, and it's where you keep your Twitter account open, then use Firefox or Internet Explorer to post from your other account. If you use the official Twitter app on your phone, then maybe use Twitterific or Tweetbot for your other account. Keeping them separate like that should help reduce any accidental postings.

The @SVHistory Twitter Account

It took Linda a couple of months of regular tweeting and following to build up a few hundred Twitter followers. She mostly used the Twitter.com website for posting blog posts, but eventually she downloaded the Twitter app onto her phone and started reading through the Twitter stream in spare moments. She began to get a sense of the people behind the accounts that she was following, and she started replying and retweeting—when it was appropriate coming from the Historical Society.

Once she tweeted a photo from the Historical Society's archives of people wearing hats that to modern eyes looked very silly and she asked for captions, for a contest. It got a huge response on Twitter, way more than she expected, and she got a big bump in followers. It even got mentioned in the Smallville *Gazette*, which wanted to post the picture, the best responses, and her choice for the winner. Linda shook her head—when did tweets become news stories?—but she sent them the picture all the same and her favorite responses.

At the beginning of every month she posted a new picture and held a new contest. It never generated the interest that the first contest did, but it was consistently popular.

Twitter was the social media site she had been the most anxious about when she started, and already it was her favorite service.

CHAPTER 5
The Email Newsletter

WITH THE SURPRISING success of her caption contest, Linda saw the viral power of social media. A single tweet was all it took, and suddenly people were talking about the Historical Society in a way she couldn't remember happening before.

The Historical Society was suddenly *interesting*.

In fact, the caption contest tweet was enough for Linda to meet her goal (and then some). When she started planning her social media strategy, she wrote down, "I will know this was successful when five strangers tell me *unasked* that they heard about us on social media."

Done!

Generally, you can't predict what will go viral. But you must be ready to capture their attention when you do.

Linda had a Constant Contact widget on her site to gather email addresses from people who wanted to subscribe to the Historical Society's newsletter, and she definitely noticed an uptick in email signups after the caption contest.

But she also realized that she hadn't sent a newsletter in almost two months. Why was she trying to collect email addresses if she wasn't using them?

When to Send Newsletters

Newsletters should be sent regularly—at least quarterly, but probably more like 6–12 times a year, depending on your organization's calendar. If you have a special reason to be sending them more often during a particular season, then send them as needed, but make sure you keep up a schedule in the off-season, just to remind readers you're around. This is especially true if you use your newsletter for a giving campaign. You can't email people only when you're asking for money, or they'll unsubscribe.

Use a Service

I strongly recommend either an email service like Constant Contact or MailChimp, or using the email feature in an integrated donor management system like the one offered by Salsa Labs. Either way, you don't want to be sending to a list from Outlook on your desktop computer. Sending hundreds of emails from a single account can get the email flagged as spam. It could even get your other non-newsletter emails flagged by certain accounts.

Using a service will reduce that issue, and it will also allow you to send an HTML newsletter that looks better than just plain text. The service is even smart enough to realize when an account doesn't accept HTML emails and will deliver them the plain text version.

Definitely use a service. The cost ranges from free to $100 a month, depending on the size of your database.

Formatting Your Newsletter

Browse through the different template options in the email management system you choose, and find one that is clean and professional. Pay attention to what you can tweak. Maybe there's a great template, but it has the wrong colors; usually that can be adjusted in the template so you can make it match your brand.

What to Send in Your Newsletter

A newsletter is much like blogging, although the posts are probably *much* shorter, since you're trying to reach someone in their inbox. Think of a newsletter as having three key parts.

The first is the key piece of information you want the reader to have: a call to give in a fall donation drive, an upcoming event, a new program announcement, a new hire. This is the primary reason you're sending the email. If you can't think of anything, you're not being creative enough. Don't be tempted to email only when you have big news. There's *something* that's going on that your donors and friends will want to know about. Put it here.

When it really comes down to it, this paragraph of your newsletter is why you've been blogging. You want people who find you through your blog and social media to opt in to your newsletter. When they do, this section is the first—and possibly only—section in the newsletter that they will read. So make it good. Edit, edit, edit until it really shines.

The next part of the newsletter is a feature. Maybe it's a blog post you've held off publishing so you could put it in the newsletter first. After you've put it in the newsletter, post it on the blog a couple of days after the newsletter comes out with the note "This post was first published in our newsletter. If you want to be the first to read it, sign up!"

Alternatively, if you don't have a blog post predrafted and really need to get your newsletter out, then select the best blog post from the last few weeks and use that as your feature, calling it out as a "can't miss" post. It's a good way to get your email subscribers who don't read blogs to be reminded of your blog's existence every so often. (If you do this, make sure you link directly to the post and not just to the blog.)

The final part of the newsletter should be something short and easy. A calendar of upcoming events for the next few months.

Or a "Did You Know?" feature with a quick fact. Or use it to thank a sponsor with a link and their logo.

Refine Your Headline

Just like for your blog post, give your headline extra attention. It probably deserves even more than a blog post headline, because for some people the headline will be the only thing they see of your newsletter, while a blog post probably has a few more indicators of whether they want to read (a photo, the first sentence).

If you had 40 other emails waiting for you, would *you* read your newsletter?

Don't Archive Your Newsletters on Your Website

I've seen many organizations do this and it never makes sense to me. It's lazy and it's frustrating for the reader.

Using the template outlined above, your newsletter has three core parts: an important news story, a feature that was or will soon be a blog post, and a short information section that contains something like upcoming events or a sponsor thank-you. *All of that should be on your website anyway.* You have a place for news (either the blog or a separate news section). You have a blog where the feature would be posted, and you have a place for events and thanking sponsors.

Archiving the newsletter duplicates content. *It's bad content.* And for readers, it's almost impossible to find the piece of information they're looking for. If your reader got your newsletter and wants to learn more about an event you posted in it, they shouldn't be forced to go through newsletter archives to figure out which issue it was mentioned in to find more information. It's way too time-consuming for them. Organize the information on your website cleanly, keep it updated, and you won't have to archive newsletters.

Don't Be Upset by Unsubscribers

Some services send you a daily or weekly list of people who have unsubscribed. Don't hold it against people who unsubscribe. They have full inboxes and busy lives. Maybe they prefer to get information via your blog or Facebook. It's not a reflection on how you've been doing or the nonprofit. Maybe they have another email address they receive your newsletter on. Don't sweat it if you see that a familiar face wants to stop receiving your newsletter, and don't harass them to find out why they unsubscribed.

CHAPTER 6
How to Evaluate New Social Media Services

SHOULD YOU BE on Foursquare? Pinterest? YouTube? Facebook and Twitter are definitely the places to start, but there might be good reasons for you to be on other social networks.

Rather than cover them all—which is impossible, since there have probably been two new social networks that have launched since you started reading this book—let's instead focus on how you might go about making that decision.

The Power of Play

The best way to determine whether a social network is good for your organization is to first determine if there's value there for *you*, as an individual. Social media at its best is for individuals. If it's useful to you as an individual, then that means people will gather there and use the service, which means there will be an audience for your nonprofit. If you can't find a good way to use the service, then maybe it's not worth the time for your organization to invest, because millions of other people will feel similarly.

So my strongest recommendation would be to sign up for the new app or website, find a couple of friends, and see if it's fun enough to use after a couple of weeks. All of these services— the good ones, anyway—try to help you get the most out of their service right at sign-up. They will show you how best to use the site. If you're still not getting something, search YouTube for videos. "How to use Pinterest" or "How to use Foursquare" show dozens of videos each.

Search on the service and look for your passions and your interests. Find things you enjoy and share them. Remember, it's *social* media. Be social, and have fun. If you like the service, then you can start thinking about how your nonprofit could use it.

(One important note: I have followed this strategy regularly. I try out social media services and then abandon them if I don't like them. I find it to be a good way to approach social media. But there is one potential negative: littering the Internet with unused social media accounts with my name all over them. When people Googled me, often some of the top hits were social media sites I no longer used. So go ahead and delete your account if you decide not to use it. You can always sign back up later if something changes.)

Deciding Whether to Use a New Social Media Service

After you've played around with a new social media service for a week or two, you probably have a good idea whether you like it. From there, you need to figure out whether there's a good reason for your nonprofit to sign up as well.

Here are some of the things worth considering:

- ***What's the basic point of the service?*** Is it to share photos? (Instagram, Flickr). Video? (YouTube, Vine, Vimeo). To share knowledge? (Quora). To share your location? (Foursquare). Knowing the basic premise is a good place to start, because it leads to the next main question:

- ***Can your nonprofit provide that service?*** If you don't have very good photos or something worth taking photographs of, or you have confidentiality issues around your nonprofit's service, maybe you shouldn't get into a photo-sharing site. If you have no videos, and no one on staff has experience making them, maybe YouTube isn't the place for you. If your nonprofit operates out of an office that people rarely visit, maybe there's no good reason to be on a location-sharing app.

- **Do you have to continue providing new content?** Some services might lend themselves to having a "presence" on them, without necessarily having to constantly maintain new content. For example, having a YouTube channel doesn't *by default* suggest that you need regularly produced content, since it's such a good place to host video. That said, most services probably do best with regular content. Can you continue to provide it? Is there a workflow that you can easily create to get new photos onto Flickr?

- **Can you fulfill your mission on the new service?** Good blogging and good use of social media are not necessarily just good marketing; they can be a good way to fulfill your mission. Would this new service help you do that in some way?

- **Does this new service put you in contact with the right people?** Are your donors on it? Are your volunteers? Are community leaders? Even if the initial use of a service isn't obvious to you, if the right people are on it, it still might be worth using, just to have another touchpoint with those people.

Case Study: Linda on Pinterest

Linda opened a Pinterest account during the Pinterest Boom of 2012 (my name for that time when it seemed as if everyone was joining Pinterest). She signed up and explored a whole world of photos and images she could pin to her boards. She created a board for design ideas, another for recipes, another of books she wanted to read, and another of travel destinations. She found her friends on there, too, and repinned their images.

Linda had enough fun on it that she suddenly wondered if she should have an account for the Historical Society. She thought about how it could work.

Pinterest was best for sharing photos of things, and most of her blog posts had photos that she owned the rights to, so she wasn't worried about having enough content. But then it would be just another place to share blog posts. Was that enough to justify signing up for a whole new account?

What could she do with Pinterest that she couldn't do on another site? She started searching Pinterest for keywords relating to the historical society, which brought up some old maps and photos, but not about anything near Smallville. What would she share?

She looked through her friend list, which was for the most part a subsection of her Facebook friends, and guessed that only about half of her friends on the service were in Smallville. Did other people in town use it much? She searched for some names but didn't see any that were closely tied to the Historical Society.

Linda eventually decided not to open a Pinterest account for the Historical Society. But on her personal account, she added a board to share blog posts and other stories about historic preservation from around the web. She decided that if it got enough attention, she would reconsider creating an account for the Historical Society. But until then, she'd stick with her own account.

I HIGHLY RECOMMEND using analytics to measure how you're doing. Yes, it's great to count followers and fans, replies and likes. But the real measures are clicks.

How many people clicked on your Twitter link? How many people clicked on the donate button after visiting your website? These are good things to know.

Tools of the Trade

The go-to application for measuring web traffic is Google Analytics. You might find another program that serves your needs better (Mint or Webtrends are two others, and there are hundreds more). But for a free service that has some great features, Google Analytics is hard to beat. Sign up for the account, and it will generate a snippet of HTML code. Just like with a YouTube video, you can paste this block of code on your website in a certain place (although it might ask you to do it in a place that you don't have access to if someone else built your site, in which case you'll have to reach out to your web developer).

Some blogging platforms have an option in which all you need to do is cut and paste in your Google Analytics account number and they put the code where it needs to be. If you have your blog hosted separately from your site, then you can use the same account for both the blog and the site. Google Analytics will treat them as one.

Using Analytics for Measuring Traffic

It can be very easy to get addicted to your analytics. You can generate graphs of practically anything, even though only a few are going to be helpful to you. Don't get sucked in to checking daily! Look at your analytics quarterly, or monthly at the most. Most of what you need in analytics reports is best understood over time. Here are the important questions to ask:

In general, how did people find your site? Your options are direct, search, or through referrals.

Direct is typing your address into the browser, clicking a bookmark, or clicking a link in an email program like Outlook.

Search is finding you via Google, Yahoo, and Bing.

Referrals measure when people click on links they find on other people's websites: Twitter, Facebook, or another link that's not on a search engine.

Depending on the specifics of your site, you may find these numbers are weighted more heavily one way than another. The numbers aren't the important part; it's their change over time that you'll want to note. Over time, if you follow the suggestions of this book, you should see your referral and direct traffic increase. This is a result of people clicking through to read your blog from Facebook and Twitter (referral traffic) and sharing links to good articles via email (direct traffic).

Both of those kinds of traffic will eventually increase your search traffic. So over time, all these kinds of traffic should increase as you blog and share links.

The breakdown within each category might be more important than the overall share. *Within search, what were the keywords people used to find you?* Are there any missing that you'd like to see? Maybe that's a topic for a new blog post?

Within referrals, where did people come from? Twitter, Facebook, a guest blog post you'd written? Maybe you should find more opportunities to write guest blog posts; maybe your Facebook account could be sending more traffic.

Your numbers will also give you a hint of what's working and what's not. The lessons you take from it are up to you. If your guest blog posts haven't worked well, is that a sign to stop them or a sign that you should do them better? That's going to be a judgment call for you to make.

Using Analytics for Improved Site Design

Analytics can help measure internal clicks as well, and here they really shine. Where do you want people to click after reading a blog post? Analytics will show you if they are doing it. If they aren't, it's a sign that perhaps the link you want them to click is in the wrong place. Or maybe it's too small and too hard to read. Google Analytics can show you the flow of visitors through a site. It can even show you a particular page on your site with information on how many clicks each link received.

Look at trends in placement: Are links in certain places more popular than others? If there's a link you really want people to click, maybe it should be near there.

Don't Base Everything on Analytics

Sometimes it's tempting to be 100% data-driven. That makes sense for Google, which once famously tested 42 different shades of blue on a single button. But your scale probably just isn't large enough to generate good enough data to base all your decisions on. A spike of 100 visitors, for a small enough nonprofit's site, could throw off all your numbers.

So balance your data-driven decisions with anecdotal information from your donors, your volunteers, or your attendees.

Conclusion

LINDA FINISHED HER three-month blogging goal and took a week off to review how things went.

She'd added a couple hundred followers to Twitter and several hundred to Facebook, and the pioneer cabin's regular patrons seemed to enjoy the Historical Society's blog. Search engine hits were up, with people discovering her blog posts, and there were now two or three new people joining the newsletter every day … instead of none.

It wasn't as far along as some of the other organizations in town, but it was a start. A start that showed the promise of what social media could do for her over the next year. In the same way that she'd set an orderly approach to fundraising, now she had a system for blogging and social media that would catch the eye of new people and bring them into a process for seeing posts, getting emails, and eventually attending, volunteering, or giving.

Better yet, she had just received a check in the mail for a membership from the mayor of Smallville. How had it happened? He wasn't on Facebook or Twitter as far as she could tell. She didn't see his email address in Constant Contact. And it had been months since she'd seen him at that dinner. What had made him join?

Linda called his office to thank him for his membership. After thanking him, she got up the courage to ask him, "I don't mean to put you on the spot, but since we met, have you been hearing about the Historical Society anywhere?"

"It seems like you've been everywhere! It's like when you learn a new word and then you can't help but notice it all the time. Three people emailed me your blog post about the Smallville bell tower. Apparently I'd been telling it all wrong. Then I saw that piece in the *Gazette* about the caption contest. I actually submitted one anonymously, but you didn't select it." He laughed and Linda joined in.

"And then there was that great blog post—your April Fool's Day interview with the first mayor of Smallville. Cracked me up!" he said. "So I started reading your blog regularly. It provides great fodder for speeches, actually. And that's when I figured I should join. To pay you back for all the ways you've helped me."

"I'm flattered that you read it!" Linda said, truly honored.

"Now, you mentioned on your blog last week that next year the cabin turns 150 years old?" the Mayor asked.

"That's right, 150 years since Thomas Winthrop started work on the cabin, the first building in Smallville," Linda answered.

"I know that the City has big ideas for our 150th anniversary, but since the cabin was built a while before incorporation, that's not for a few more years yet. We should be able to do something to commemorate the cabin next year. How do you feel about a day of proclamation?"

"We would love that!" Linda exclaimed.

"If you put together some festivities, let me know that too. I'd love to be there to welcome everyone," the Mayor said.

"We definitely will," she said.

"Here, let me give you the direct number for my assistant. As soon as you have a date, let her know and she'll make sure it's on my calendar."

As she wrote down the contact information, Linda felt that her smile could be seen across the phone connection. "Thank you, Mr. Mayor. It would be an honor to have you at the celebration, and I'm so glad that you decided to join the Historical Society."

Was this book helpful to you?

PLEASE CONSIDER LEAVING a review online to help other small nonprofit managers find this resource as well!

You can also sign up here to receive more information from Erik Hanberg about all facets of small nonprofit management: http://bit.ly/forsmallnonprofitsemail

(We will *never* sell or give away your email address to a third party)

Technology Resource Guide

BELOW IS A short description of some of the technological tools mentioned in this guide, as well as some that weren't but may still be good to understand.

Social Media and Blogging Tools

Blogger: The easiest way to start a blog. But easiest doesn't always mean best. Its customization options aren't as good as others'. But if you truly have no technical skills, Blogger will make it as easy as possible for you.

Facebook: With more than 1 billion users, Facebook is far and away the largest social network. If there's any network you can assume by default that someone is on, it's this one.

Flickr: A popular photo-sharing site. A great archive of online photos, it could be a place to store your hi-res photos without having to host them on your own site. If you need photos to illustrate blog posts, you can also search for photos that have "Creative Commons" licenses and use them without having to pay, as long as you give attribution to the photographer. The site is flickr.com/creativecommons to search these photos.

Foursquare: A popular location-sharing network. If you have a physical office or run a business or a place people attend, such as a theater, you will definitely want to make sure you are ready for people to "check in" on Foursquare. You can offer deals and discounts to people who check in.

Google+: Google's gone social. As of this writing, the network is smaller than Facebook's, but it has some features that Facebook doesn't have, like video chat (called "Hangouts") where people can interact with each other or listen to a central speaker. Also, Google+ is tightly integrated with Google Search, which may be the best reason to have a presence on it right now.

Instagram: If you have a smartphone, you can use Instagram. It's an easy way to share photos and apply filters to them to make them look vintage or otherwise artistic. It works only from a phone, so the user base is smaller than that of some networks. But it's easy to share photos from your phone to Facebook and Twitter from the app.

Pinterest: A place to "pin" photos and videos to boards, sorted by category.

Tumblr: A popular blog site, Tumblr makes it easy for your followers to re-share your posts. The downside is that sometimes it can be hard to tell where a post originated, so your great post might be great, but the credit back to you could be lost.

Twitter: A real-time information network. A smaller network than Facebook, it nevertheless has strong potential for you to broadcast news and information to a dedicated fanbase.

Vimeo: A common alternative to YouTube. The premium version has some features YouTube doesn't. But it's not owned by Google, so it's likely not as tightly knitted with Google search results.

WordPress: An out-of-the-box blogging solution that is mostly free. You can buy templates and easily customize them. It takes some knowledge of how websites work if you don't want a domain name with WordPress in it, but some tutorials will get you where you want to go.

YouTube: The most popular video sharing site. If you have videos, you should consider hosting them with YouTube so they are easily found by people searching it. It's another way for people to discover you.

Helpful Nonsocial Technology

Bluehost.com: My favorite hosting site. Costs are less than $110 for a year of hosting and registering a domain name.

Constant Contact: A paid email management system. Very common and trusted by consumers (among those who notice, at least). There's a stock of templates to adapt as needed. It's a paid service, so expect to pay at least $20 to $50 per month depending on the size of your email list.

Eventbrite: An easy way to handle event RSVPs. You can have paid tickets or free tickets and choose whether to pass the fee on to customers or factor it in to the ticket price. Pays within a week after the event via direct deposit. No charge outside of the fees per paid ticket.

eTapestry: An online donor database. There's a free version but unless you really understand donor databases, it will be hard to use. It's run by a publicly traded company, Blackbaud, which also owns the incredibly expensive Raiser's Edge database. I do think it's odd that a huge publicly traded company has a near monopoly on donor databases for nonprofits, so I can't say I totally recommend it. But you should know of eTapestry.

Google Analytics: A great service for measuring Web traffic that is also free. A lot of data and other information can be mined from here.

MailChimp: Unlike Constant Contact, you can use MailChimp for free if you have fewer than 2,000 email addresses or send fewer than 12,000 emails a month. In exchange, I would say it's *slightly* harder to use if you're not that technically inclined.

PayPal: A standard payment gateway that most people already have an account for. It's not the best system, but it's very common for people to have an account with PayPal already.

Salsa Labs: A donor database and communications tool specifically for nonprofits. I highly recommend their work.

Square: I love Square. It's an easy way to swipe credit cards at an event. Fast and a great rate. It also seems to delight customers who haven't signed with a touchscreen before. Fast deposit of money into your account. A great tool to have on hand.

Non-Fiction
The Little Book of Gold: Fundraising for Small (and Very Small) Nonprofits

Arthur Beautyman Mysteries
The Saints Go Dying
The Marinara Murders
The Con Before Christmas

Science Fiction
The Lead Cloak

About the Author

Erik Hanberg has spent years working for nonprofits.

He's worked in marketing and fundraising for nonprofits in economic development, the arts, and education. He's been the director of two nonprofits: the Grand Cinema, an art-house movie theater, and City Club of Tacoma, a civic nonprofit. Hanberg has sat on boards of many organizations and now helps give money to nonprofits through his role on the Distribution Committee of the Greater Tacoma Community Foundation.

Along with his wife, a professional graphic designer, Hanberg runs a boutique marketing company that specializes in nonprofit marketing, social media, and publishing.

Find him online at:
www.forsmallnonprofits.com
www.erikhanberg.com
or on Twitter at @erikhanberg

80701267R00059

Made in the USA
Columbia, SC
20 November 2017